Beloved and Betrayed

how nine miners, a clerk and a bricklayer shocked the football world

John Stocks and Lance Hardy

First published by JVS Publishing in 2023

Printed in the UK by
221Creative,
1 Wallace Road, Sheffield S3 7AR
https://www.221print.com

All rights reserved

© John Stocks and Lance Hardy, 2023

The right of John Stocks and Lance Hardy to be identified as author of this work has been asserted in accordance with Section 77 of the Copyright, Designs and Patents Act 1988.

This book is sold subject to the condition that it shall not, by way of trade or otherwise, be lent, resold, hired out or otherwise circulated without the publisher's prior consent in any form of binding or cover other that that in which it is published and without a similar condition including this condition being imposed on the subsequent purchaser.

A CIP record for this book is available from the British Library.

ISBN   978 1 7397930 1 2

Beloved and Betrayed

how nine miners, a clerk and a bricklayer shocked the football world

Authors: John Stocks and Lance Hardy

Cover Design: Diane Moxon

Text and Internal Design: Dave Pickersgill

Images:

Richard Allsopp (RA), Bassetlaw Museum (BM), G Blundell (GB), Caseldine Family (CF), Daily Mail Archive (DM), Stuart Dickenson (SD), Mavis Froggatt (MF), Bob Goodwin (BG), Mike Holmes (MH), Inspire Culture, Learning and Libraries (includes Worksop Library) (IC), Lord Mann Collection (LM), Frank Newnes commission (FN), Photographer unknown (n/k), L Richardson (LR), Alan Rolfe (AR), Sunday Pictorial/Mirrorpix (SP), Taylor Company Archive (TC), Worksop Guardian (WG) and Paul Wyer (PW)

Back cover image of John and Lance: Mike Holmes

Acknowledgements:

Richard Allsopp, Bassetlaw Museum, Caseldine Family, Devon Cash, James Dutton, Helen Fox, Bob Goodwin, Adelle Hardy, Inspire Culture, Learning and Libraries, Steve Jarvis, Lord Mann, Diane Moxon, Dave Pickersgill, Ian Preece, Phil Whitehead and Worksop Town FC

Everyone involved in the production of 'Beloved and Betrayed' has given their time freely. Any financial surplus accrued will, in Lance Hardy's name, be given to an appropriate charity.

Contents

Introduction 1

Prologue 3
    Worksop 5:00 pm. Saturday, January 13th 1923.
    Working-Class Heroes.

1. 'Bill Lilley. A Born Footballer.' 5
    December 6th 1919.
    Anthem for Doomed Youth.

2. August 1919. A Hero Betrayed. 9
    A Childhood Dream is Realised.
    Mustard Gas in the Dead of Night.
    Saturday April 5th 1920. Redemption.

3. Welcome to Worksop. 15
    1861
    Founding Fathers.

4. Tottenham Hotspur. A village in Middlesex. 21
    Harry Hotspur.

5. A Modern World. 22
    Alderman Charles Arthur Longbottom (1864-1935).

6. Worksop Town. Midland League Champions. 25
    The power of Wireless and Looping the Loop.
    Mansfield Again. A Nottinghamshire Derby.

7. October 1922. Worksop's FA Cup Campaign. 28
    Fourth Qualifying Round. Scunthorpe United. Home.
    Fifth Qualifying Round. Grimsby Town. Away.
    Sixth Qualifying Round. Chesterfield. Home.
    Mixed Reactions.

8. Chelsea. 34

9. Goliath v David. 37
    'The past is another country,
    they do things differently there.'   LP Hartley.
    A Small Town Team with a Big Heart.

10. London Calling. 42
    Tottenham Hotspur v Worksop Town.
            Saturday, January 13th 1923
    Living the Dream.
    Lest we Forget.
    'Nothing to lose. Everything to gain.'

11. Tom Richardson and his Merry Men. 49
    Full-Backs.
    Half-Backs.
    Forwards.
    If only.

12. George Watkinson and the Herbert Chapman factor.
                                                    60
    WM.

13. London's finest. 64
    Full-Backs.
    Half-backs.
    Forwards. The Famous Five.
    The Boss.

14. Destiny Calls. 71
    Hewers and Heroes.
    Worksop play the WM.
    Hewers and Heroes. Second Half.

15. Glory Boys. The Magnificent Miners. 80
    Hindsight is a Wonderful Thing.

16.	Triumph and Disaster.	84
	The Tottenham Hotspur Office. White Hart Lane 4.30pm.	
	The Dressing Room. White Hart Lane 5.30pm.	
17.	Saturday Night and Sunday Morning.	89
	Piccadilly. Saturday, January 13th 10.30pm.	
	Worksop Station. Sunday, January 14th 2am.	
	The Imperial Hotel, Sunday, January 14th 11am.	
18.	Aftermath.	90
	The Deal.	
	Taking Chance Out of the Equation.	
19.	Tottenham Hotspur v Worksop Town (replay).	94
	White Hart Lane. Monday January 15th 2.30pm.	
	Homeward Bound. Monday, January 15th 7pm.	
20.	The Game that Might Have Been.	97
	Hanging Together.	
21.	The Road to Wembley.	101
22.	A third betrayal and an unlikely reunion.	104
	Jack and Jimmy save the Owls.	
	Up the Owls.	
23.	If Only We'd had Spink. Part Two.	107
24.	Oblivion.	110
	What Became of the Likely Lads?	
	The Long and Winding Road.	
25.	Immortal Memory.	114
	References and Further Reading.	116

Introduction

Sometimes ordinary people can achieve extraordinary things. As a small boy, growing up in north Nottinghamshire, Lance Hardy could not have dreamed, as he watched his first FA Cup final in 1973, when Second Division Sunderland unexpectedly beat a great Leeds United side, that he was destined to write the definitive book on that game.

After watching the game on television, at his family home on Kilton Hill, Worksop, Lance became a life-long Sunderland supporter. His book, *'Stokoe, Sunderland and '73,'* was shortlisted for Football Book of the Year in 2010 at the British Sports Book Awards. It remains, arguably, the greatest book ever written about Sunderland football club, continuing, world-wide, to capture the hearts of fans of the Black Cats.

Lance's early career was as a reporter on the *Worksop Trader*, and then Group Editor, whilst studying journalism at Richmond College in Sheffield. He moved to London in 1990, starting at BBC Ceefax, before working on several BBC Sport national institutions: *Football Focus, Final Score, Match of the Day*, World Cups and Olympic Games. He also wrote many other successful sports books.

Lance made an indelible impression on everyone who met him. His wit, positivity and generosity enriched the lives of many, and his zest for life and adventure was infectious.

Lance and I bonded over a story that was handed down from our grandfathers, about another football team. The story of how nine coal miners, a clerk, and a bricklayer from what the London press referred to as 'a small pit village that no one had heard of' shocked the football world in January 1923. We researched the story together and grew to love the 'Boys of '23,' admiring their courage, humour, and spirit.

This was the second football story, equally close to his heart, that Lance was destined to write. When Lance learned that his time on Earth was to end prematurely, one of his dying wishes was that I should complete the project, and publish the book in both our names, using Lance's title, *Beloved and Betrayed*. It has been an honour and privilege to do so.

John Stocks   johnstocks1861@gmail.com

Beloved and Betrayed

Prologue

Worksop 5:00 pm. Saturday, January 13th 1923.

A visitor to Worksop alighting from their train in the twilight would have seen nothing that was untoward in the coal-smoked town. The wheels of industry continued to turn. The collieries, part of a vast, sprawling coalfield that stretched from the West Riding of Yorkshire to Derbyshire and north Nottinghamshire, were as busy as ever.

It was a noisy old place. Coal waggons shunted up and down, clanging as they coupled and uncoupled. Pit-head winding wheels turned, and a plethora of chimneys belched smoke. On the fringes of the town, black-faced miners could be seen carrying 'snap cans' as they moved to and from their places of employment.

It was a brew-day at the huge Worksop and Retford Brewery which loomed over the town. The mashing grains and boiling added to the sensory overload. Rich scents of hops and sweet malt mingled with the acrid tang of coal-smoke.

The real action was underground where colliers, often called hewers, were using hand-held picks to break coal from the Top Hard seam (aka the Barnsley Bed or Barnsley Main) – then the most sought-after seam of coal due to its excellent steam-raising qualities. Others were shovelling coal into tubs which were pulled by ponies along temporary roadways.

Many of the young men were as lean and fit as athletes, with sinews tightened and muscles toned by physical labour. It was said that you 'only had to whistle down a pit' and a fast bowler or centre-forward would emerge, ready to take on the best.

However, others were broken. Old well before their three score years and ten. The work was hard and back breaking, with the slow killer of lung disease and arthritis knocking decades off life expectancies. Conditions and face-height varied from colliery to colliery and the threat of disaster from explosions, roof falls and water ingress were ever present.

If our visitor chose to linger a while, they may have noticed that there were broad smiles on the faces of numerous groups of people who stood gossiping on street corners. The pubs and clubs appeared to be full, and men lucky enough to have finished their day shift had a glint in their eye and a spring in their step.

Working-Class Heroes.

When Worksop Town of the Midland League, an association football team of miners from that 'small pit village that no one had heard of' (according to one member of the London press), had been drawn to play against 'England's Premier Team' of the day, Tottenham Hotspur, the *London Daily News* announced that the FA Cup draw 'was met with a loud burst of laughter.' The *Daily Mirror* declared that the underdogs chances were 'practically nil,' and the Worksop team were advised to, 'take a cricket book to record the score.'

However, on a Saturday afternoon of mist and lingering frost on a half-frozen pitch, nine miners who had been working a full shift as late as Thursday, aided by a clerk and a bricklayer, were destined to become headline news across the British Empire. It was a miracle to some, a fairy story to others: a moment even more beautiful and memorable for being so unexpected by all except those who knew the special qualities of their 'collier boys.'

It was a feat that elicited tears of joy and prompted grown men and women, old enough to know better, to dance impromptu jigs in the street. The pubs on Worksop's ancient thoroughfare Bridge Street, and elsewhere, did a roaring trade. People were heard to remark that it was 'busier than Christmas Eve' in the smoky tap rooms and snugs.

Small children, some carrying stuffed toy Tigers, the mascot of the Worksop Town football team, would be given special dispensation to join the merry throng heading to the railway station. They would share in the magical moment when the working-class heroes of White Hart Lane were welcomed home and carried shoulder-high through the streets of Worksop.

The supporters who had not been lucky enough to travel down on the Saturday Special, or with the official party in the hired saloons attached to the engine that had steamed its way to Retford on Friday morning, joining the London Express, were waiting in the freezing cold on Platform One of Worksop's railway station. It was 2.15 am on Sunday morning and they stood patiently, gazing through the freezing mist, hoping to catch a glimpse of the puffs of smoke that would herald the arrival of the heavily loaded mail train from north London, and the men who would soon alight from it.

As it steamed west, past the final signal box, a mighty cheer echoed from the faithful supporters. Many waved caps and hats in the air in time honoured fashion.

When the mail train finally came to a halt, each one of them seemed to subconsciously hold their breath as they eagerly awaited the moment when the doors would open.

That feeling of anticipation was quickly replaced by the sudden and sobering realisation that nobody was getting off the train.

The rumours had been true after all.

The players were not coming home.

The mood quickly became as dark as the sky above.

The joy and wonder felt moments earlier passed away.

It would never return, but neither would it ever be forgotten.

100 years on, it is still remembered.

1. 'Bill Lilley. A Born Footballer.'

December 6th 1919.

Bill Lilley wheeled his bike out of the outhouse at 9am. After finishing his shift at Wombwell Colliery he had elected to have a lie-in before cycling the 22 miles direct to the Elland Road ground, Leeds, rather than riding to Worksop to join his teammates. This was a slight deviation from his usual Saturday routine. If the team were travelling by train or charabanc, he would cycle a similar distance to join his comrades at Worksop. It had been a busy week. Supplying coke for iron works all over Yorkshire and into Nottinghamshire from the Barnsley, Parkgate and Silkstone seams, Wombwell Colliery was still enjoying a lingering wartime boom.

An ex-school teacher, unable to return to his profession after the war, Bill's thoughts may have strayed to the east. The news was dominated by reports of the Red Army of Soviet Russia inflicting defeats on the Ukrainian People's Republic and Estonia. Only recently back from a traumatic time on the Western Front, Bill did not like the thought of someone needlessly starting another European conflict.

Considered to be the final conflict, the 'War to end all Wars' was still delivering casualties, victims of lingering sepsis or acute psychological trauma. The year would see many ex-soldiers take their own lives. The sniper's bullet did not distinguish between a miner and part-time footballer playing in the Midland League or a cosseted professional from the elite division of the greatest footballing nation on earth. War was a great leveller.

As if to accentuate the prevailing mood of grief and sombre reflection, December had opened with a spell of mild, wet and dull weather with frequent gales. Manchester only recorded seven hours of sunshine during the whole of December. Bill put his cape over his shoulders and fastened his bicycle clips before he set off. His boots were tucked into his saddle bag.

In 1915 William Lilley had been a Sheffield man, working as a schoolmaster, but dreaming of a career in football. He was faced with the daunting task of trying to rise to the top in an area filled to the brim with high-quality competitive teams and raw young talent. *The Star Green 'Un*, Sheffield's top sports paper with plenty of exceptional players to compare him against, described Bill as a 'born footballer' (October 9th 1915). His 'dash, determination and physique' were impossible to ignore and Worksop Town, with its fine track record of producing or refining first-class footballers before selling them on to the biggest clubs in the land, was the ideal place for him to showcase his skills.

At the start of 1915, the year that Sheffield United won the biggest prize in the land defeating Chelsea 3-0 in the Khaki cup final, so called because so many spectators were already in uniform, Lilley, signed from Wombwell in 1913, was on the fast track to top-flight football. Scouts from Sheffield United and their great rivals Wednesday were tracking Bill Lilley's every move.

He made an instant impact in the Midland League with Worksop: by February 1914 Lilley had scored 12 goals in 18 appearances. As, *The*

Green 'Un starkly observed, the bidding only stopped 'because of the crisis into which the world was plunged.'

Lilley had helped his cause by scoring a wonder goal against Wednesday Reserves in a superb performance that gave Worksop their first win over the Owls since 1908. He had followed up with a dominant performance in a 3-0 victory against a Sheffield United Reserve team containing first-team regulars Kitchen, Hawley and Revill. Pre-war reports highlight his shooting technique, the power of his shots, his limitless energy, and his physicality.

The pressure for a local school teacher to join the patriotic fight for king and country was immense, and in 1915 Lilley sacrificed the prospect of a career in the top flight for the challenge of the Western Front. Here he would face the terror of attack by poison gas administered by the German Army (at Valenciennes in France). As a school master it is possible his attention would have later been drawn to Wilfred Owen's harrowing poem.

Anthem for Doomed Youth.

>Bent double, like old beggars under sacks,
>
>Knock-kneed, coughing like hags, we cursed through sludge,
>
>Till on the haunting flares we turned our backs
>
>And towards our distant rest began to trudge.
>
>Men marched asleep. Many had lost their boots
>
>But limped on, blood-shod. All went lame; all blind;
>
>Drunk with fatigue; deaf even to the hoots
>
>Of tired, outstripped Five-Nines that dropped behind.
>
>Gas! Gas! Quick, boys!—An ecstasy of fumbling,
>
>Fitting the clumsy helmets just in time;
>
>But someone still was yelling out and stumbling
>
>And flound'ring like a man in fire or lime...
>
>Dim, through the misty panes and thick green light,

Beloved and Betrayed

> As under a green sea, I saw him drowning.
>
> In all my dreams, before my helpless sight,
> He plunges at me, guttering, choking, drowning.
>
> If in some smothering dreams you too could pace
> Behind the wagon that we flung him in,
> And watch the white eyes writhing in his face,
> His hanging face, like a devil's sick of sin;
> If you could hear, at every jolt, the blood
> Come gargling from the froth-corrupted lungs,
> Obscene as cancer, bitter as the cud
> Of vile, incurable sores on innocent tongues -
> My friend, you would not tell with such high zest
> To children ardent for some desperate glory,
> The old Lie: *Dulce et decorum est Pro patria mori.*

William Lilley was to be left with another daily reminder of his time in the trenches. When he played his final pre-war game for the Worksop club, he had a full head of hair. Severe concussion triggered by an artillery bombardment led to premature baldness. On his return, still a relatively young man in his mid-twenties, he would have to accept the affectionate appellation 'Old Bill' from the supporters of his home-town club and 'Grandad' or 'Baldy' from less sympathetic rivals. The Sheffield teams were no longer interested in a player with gas-scarred lungs.

It was a callous and cynical rejection, and it was manifestly wrong. Bill could still play football, as he would prove on a murky December afternoon in Leeds.

Leeds City had been a force in the Football League. In October 1919, they were compulsory wound up by order of a joint FA and Football

League commission after the club refused to open its accounts. They were swiftly re-incarnated as Leeds United and were expected to dominate the Midland League, before joining the football league in their second season.

Worksop opened the game attacking the terracing at the Gelderd Road end of Leeds United's impressive ground, and soon had the Leeds United defenders pinned back in their own half as Worksop Town launched a series of spirited attacks. United, in their black and white striped shirts, were struggling to cope with sweeping attacks launched down both wings. Ted 'Raz' Lindley and Bill were in outstanding form as Worksop Town completely outclassed Leeds, winning 5-3.

Worksop went on to win the return game at Central Avenue, becoming the first team to do the double over Leeds United. Their 100% record against Leeds United in competitive games still stands. The result was the first intimation that Worksop Town were building an exciting team, and that Bill Lilley would be part of it.

2.   August 1919. A Hero Betrayed.

As the train chugged along the Rhondda Valley, Jimmy Seed's heart sank as soon as the pit stacks and spoil heaps came into view. It was a painful reminder of the world he was trying to escape from. Jimmy, born and raised on the Durham coalfield had become a collier boy on leaving school. He had hated mining from the start and had been determined to forge a life for himself above ground.

Jimmy had heard of Tonypandy. It was a name that was etched into the folklore of all mining communities after the Tonypandy riots of 1911. The riots were a series of tumultuous confrontations between striking miners and the police. The clashes intensified as an industrial dispute between the colliers and the Cambrian Combine (a cartel of private mine owners who controlled prices and wages) intensified. After fist fights between miners from the wider Rhondda Valley and the Glamorgan Constabulary, reinforcements were brought in from Bristol to bolster the beleaguered Welsh policemen.

Winston Churchill, as Home Secretary, controversially ordered the British Army to assist in the struggle in which a miner, Samuel Rhys, was killed. The story of how he died evolved into an urban myth that he was shot and killed by the troops after Churchill had suggested that the soldiers 'fill their bellies with lead.' This led to Churchill becoming an unpopular figure in mining communities across the land. Whilst both the event and Churchill's words are falsely reported, the equally unpalatable truth for the victim's family, was that Rhys was killed by a violent blow to the head.

For Seed and his teammate Frank Pattison, the sight of the scarred industrial valley, and the prospect of Second Division Southern League football, represented heartache and cruel rejection.

Jimmy Seed was cut from the same rich seam as the Worksop miners from Manton Colliery. He was from a north-eastern mining family. Originally from Blackhill in County Durham, by 1897, two years after Jimmy was born, the family had settled in Whitburn, a coastal village three miles north of Sunderland. Mining had been a way of life for generations. Excelling at football was the only realistic escape from the drudgery and misery of the miner's lot: The risks posed by the inhalation of coal dust and the ever-present threats of maiming, mutilation and death.

With educational opportunities restricted, football was the only practical means of escape. Seed was blessed with exceptional talent. Football was the principal recreation for coal-mining lads and, like many, Seed grew up playing and watching football with his four brothers and five sisters. He was a Sunderland supporter, and his team were one of the greatest teams in the world.

After his older siblings allowed him to tag along to games, he became a fan of the 'Mackems.' 'The giants of soccer came and went as week after week I went to Roker Park, but the man who held my attention longer than any among my schoolboy heroes was Charlie Buchan. His tricks and subtle moves impressed me so much that I would spend hours trying to copy him. I didn't wait until I arrived home. The lesson began as soon as I had turned down some side street to avoid the crowd. Then for two miles, with the help of a small rubber ball, I would attempt to reproduce the latest Buchan move.'

However, the opportunity to sign professional forms with a local football club, remained a dream for many, achieved only by an exceptional minority. Living within walking distance of what he described as 'England's richest soccer nursery' at Roker Park gave Seed an advantage on 'the soccer trail' but he would have to outpace hundreds of others on the same path.

Jimmy had been a talented and capable student at school, excelling at art and music and his parents discussed whether it might be possible for him to train as a teacher. In later years Jimmy would entertain his teammates by playing modern ragtime on the piano, or by drawing professional-looking sketches and caricatures that were regularly published, alongside his articles.

For now, like the nine Worksop miners, he was expected to do his bit to put bread on the table. Leaving school at 14 he was old enough to sign up to work as a pit boy at the Whitburn Colliery, initially working as a trapper, opening and closing the wooden doors that allowed a free flow of fresh air through the mine. Later he progressed to driver, driving the ponies that pulled the coal carts on the main tunnels which led to the coalface. He would walk to and from the colliery in Marsden, just north of Whitburn, and was expected to work mainly night shifts. At the age of 16 he became a hewer. From the outset he hated life in the mine.

If a chance of escape came it had to be taken. With so many desperate to find an alternative to underground toil, taking part in training and the subsequent 'trial' could be a once in a lifetime opportunity. However, Seed's was destined to be a catastrophic failure. He waited nervously outside the main entrance of Roker Park and only plucked up courage to enter when a friend arrived. They went in together. At his subsequent trial, wearing borrowed boots that were too big and exhausted after completing a full night shift at the colliery, Jimmy was forced to play out of position as a centre-forward.

Devastated by his hapless performance, Seed thought the gates of Roker Park had closed on him forever. For a young man who hated coal-mining, and the experience of working underground, it was a huge disappointment. 'I did nothing and realised as I dressed after the trial in readiness for another night shift, that Sunderland would not be interested in me,' said Jimmy.

He was mistaken. Such was the scale of Seed's skill set, goal-scoring expertise and flair that his impressive exploits as a teenager with

Whitburn's first-team were impossible to ignore, and a rare second chance followed. This time, playing in his best role as an inside-forward, Jimmy scored a hat-trick in a sublime and mature performance. Aged just 19, Seed had the precious contract in his pocket. 'I was thrilled to sign professional forms for the side that had been known as the Team of all the Talents, one of the biggest clubs in the land.'

A Childhood Dream is Realised.

Arriving at Sunderland just as Worksop's Walter Scott left, Jimmy was about to become a junior teammate of Sunderland's greatest ever striker, Charlie Buchan, and of a Worksop-born Sunderland defensive legend, Charlie Gladwin.

Although Buchan had started his career in 1909 with Woolwich Arsenal (later renamed Arsenal FC), his greatest achievements came as part of the Sunderland 'Team of all the Talents.' Buchan was leading scorer for seven of his nine seasons with the club and he set goal-scoring records that have yet to be surpassed. He remains Sunderland's all-time leading goal-scorer. Buchan was a winner of the First Division title in 1913 and reached the FA Cup Final with Sunderland in the same year.

Awarded the Military Medal after fighting with the Sherwood Foresters in World War One, he became an Arsenal player in the post-war era, under Herbert Chapman. He went on to play for England and became even more famous because of his association with *Charles Buchan's Football Monthly* magazine.

One of the finest players Worksop football has ever produced, 'the Sunderland Colossus,' Charlie Gladwin, six-foot-one-inch, 14 stone, granite jawed enforcer and right-back, born in Worksop in 1887, joined Blackpool directly from local football. Gladwin subsequently went on to become a dominant force in defence as Sunderland won the First Division title.

Charlie Buchan recalled that 'Sunderland became a first-class team from the moment he [Gladwin] joined the side. Not only did we win the League Championship with a record number of points, but we nearly brought off the elusive League and Cup double, accomplished only by Preston North End and Aston Villa. There are people who say that no one player can make a poor side into a great one and that there isn't one worth a £3,000 transfer fee. Gladwin proved they are wrong.'

Gladwin, who did not suffer fools gladly, removed a Newcastle fan who had insulted him after a derby against Sunderland, off a tram with one punch, holding his precious boots under the other arm!

It is not clear whether Jimmy spent time with these luminaries of pre-war football. He had to learn his trade in the reserves. Initially, despite the physique and physical strength that he had already acquired from mining, he found the training arduous and struggled to keep pace with the First Division professionals.

But Seed was making progress and heading for a first-team place when war broke out in 1914. Sadly, he would never play for his beloved Sunderland.

Mustard Gas in the Dead of Night.

By 1915, with pressure mounting on players and spectators alike (in Sunderland, Lord Durham even said that he wished the Germans would drop bombs on Roker Park to encourage men to think about where they should be), Jimmy had reached the age when he was old enough to be called to serve in the Great War.

Assigned to the Northern Cycling Corps, Jimmy was sent to Gainsborough, near Worksop, to train. Effectively he was to be a delivery boy, but a delivery boy who faced daily risks that transcended those he had faced in the mine. Remarkably, Jimmy Seed would survive two attacks by poison gas, one cloud administered by the German Army, the other delivered by the German Air Force. His grandson vividly describes the first attack in his blog:

'In the early hours of July 22nd 1917, Jimmy was one of many soldiers gassed in Nieuwpoort, near Ostend. The attack, one of the earliest utilising mustard gas, hospitalised 802 soldiers, 96 of whom died. Jimmy was sheltering in the basement of a bombed-out building with his comrades when mustard gas shells were dropped from German aeroplanes in the dead of night. Being heavier than air the gas seeped down into their cellar, their confinement meaning the attack was far more deadly than it would normally have been in the open air.

One of the lucky ones to survive from that group, Jimmy was sent home to convalesce after a two-week hospitalisation in Belgium, but it's unclear whether he was hospitalised in England as well or was able to go home to Whitburn to recover. Either way, it would be a full 13 months before he was well enough to return to action, such was the severity of the damage to his lungs.'

With the callous indifference and contempt that characterised the personal management of clubs at the time, when Jimmy reported for duty at Roker Park, he discovered that, instead of being welcomed back with open arms to the club that he had cherished as a boy, he had been commodified. Fearing that his gas-scarred lungs would no longer function adequately enough for him to give the club value for money, Sunderland had let him go. This was the first of two great betrayals, both of which would leave more lasting scars than the Kaiser's gas. He would resume his career at non-League Mid Rhondda.

He did not know it at the time, but the Rhondda was a valley that would soon lead to his salvation. His welcome augured well, as he explained in his biography: 'As soon as I got off the train, I was cheered like as if I was a heavyweight champion of the world, rather than a reject who had been told his footballing days were over.'

Saturday April 5th 1920. Redemption.

Jimmy Seed alighted at Tonypandy railway station with his boots in hand and the best wishes of the supporters who had travelled with him on the Taff Vale line still ringing in his ears. The standard gauge railway in south Wales, built by the Taff Vale Railway Company to serve the iron and coal industries around Merthyr Tydfil, and provide access to the docks at Cardiff, had been thick with pipe and cigarette smoke. Rugby Union and Association Football players and supporters joked and joshed as they were thrown together, the overcrowded train rattling ominously down the old line.

Jimmy was already a popular figure in south Wales, conspicuously orchestrating the midfield at Mid Rhondda, bitterly determined to demonstrate the stupidity of Sunderland's decision to dismiss him. The power of his running and his seemingly limitless energy belied the assumption that his lungs had been ravaged by poison gas.

The rugby obsessed heartland of south Wales was not the ideal place to showcase his sublime skillset, but soccer fever had gripped the local population and Seed was about to get a well-deserved stroke of fortune. Peter McWilliam, the famous Tottenham Hotspur manager was covertly attending a Ton Pentre v Mid-Rhondda game in disguise; not to watch Jimmy Seed, but to cast a discerning eye on a player called Lowdell, who was representing Ton Pentre.

An astute assessor of footballing potential, McWilliam found his attention drifting away from Lowdell towards a commanding dark-haired midfielder. A similar player in style to Johnny Giles, the star of a great Leeds United side many years later, Seed was adept at finding space and comfortable at holding the ball until he could spot the perfect pass.

By half-time McWilliam had made up his mind. He would invest his chairman's money, not on Lowdell (who would eventually become a Spurs player) but on Jimmy Seed. It was one of the defining moments in Jimmy's colourful career.

A natural leader of men by talent and example, he was destined to become the creative engine of a new 'team of all the talents.' Sunderland's loss was Spurs' gain.

3.   Welcome to Worksop.

When Worksop FC was first born it was to a very small town of around 7,000 inhabitants. A town surrounded by ducal estates - a rural, agricultural backwater whose main industries were malting, milling and timber production.

Descriptions of the town of Worksop before the sinking of the collieries invariably suggest that it was something of a semi-rural idyll. The historian, Mr Eddison, writing in 1854, describes, 'a pleasant, cheerful looking town of well-built houses and wide commodious streets.'

However, by the turn of the 20th century the nature of the town was very different. It was now a grimy, noisy, industrial powerhouse, with a skyline dominated by smoke stacks, colliery headgears, smouldering spoil tips and an ever-growing population. Between the years of 1891 and 1911 the population of Worksop increased from 12,700 to 20,300.

The Industrial Revolution had been propelled by one major resource, coal. By 1900 the country's steel-mills, foundries, power stations, railways, ship builders, domestic users and export traders were ever hungry for vast quantities of coal – the country's most vital natural resource.

Worksop was no exception to this dash for coal as more local collieries opened. The pioneering enterprise that had been Shireoaks Colliery (sunk in 1854) had been followed by many other local collieries: Kiveton (1866) Barlborough (1873) Steetley (1873), Southgate (1875) Markam (1882) and Whitwell (1890). During the course of the latter 19th century many more pits had been developed in the near wider area, such as Bolsover (1891), Warsop Main (1893) Creswell (1894) and Shirebrook (1896).

At the dawn of the 20th century these were joined by the massive new development by the Wigan Coal & Iron Co. (WC&I Co.) at Manton Wood in Worksop, and a huge influx of miners from Lancashire. Other collieries within travelling distance opened, including Dinnington Main (1902) and Thurcroft (circa 1905).

1861

Winston Churchill once defined Russia as 'a riddle, wrapped in a mystery , inside an enigma.' He could have been speaking about the history of Worksop FC (later Worksop Town FC). His words would have resonated with the reporter from the *Sunday Illustrated* dispatched in January 1923 to the frozen north, to spend the night in a provincial hotel, with instructions to find out more about the story of 'the proud pit village' that no one in the capital had heard of.

Technically, Worksop did not become a town until 1931 when it received an official charter. It was a village where the men had the audacity to think they could take on London's finest and seriously believe that they could beat them.

The unnamed journalist gave it his best shot, interviewing dozens of talkative locals and delivering enough copy for a full-page spread, but he found the story of the history of Worksop FC lost in the mists of time and the club records apparently destroyed by one of the regular floods and inundations, that left the town grounds and offices submerged in six feet of stinking water from the River Ryton, popularly known as 'the Town-Dyke.'

'It is not surprising that the club were a mystery to London, for in some ways they were a mystery to themselves,' wrote the journalist. No one seemed to know anything about the origins or the foundation year of the club. The moment lived only in legends and romantic stories, all attached to a foundation date, 1861.

However, Worksop was far from being a football backwater. Set between the early footballing heartlands of Sheffield and Nottingham, with close business, social and sporting associations with the former city, Worksop, from the beginning, was snug in the cradle of what would become the global game. For 50 years it had been on a steep learning curve, developing a rich football culture and a large cohort of professional players who had excelled on the national stage.

The earliest surviving club minutes 1911-23 (LM)

1861 is the date hand-written and typed on the earliest surviving set of minutes, 1911-1914 series (a semi-legal document). The header reads: 'The Worksop Town Football Club formed in 1861.' It also appears, unquestioned and undisputed by their bitterest early rivals Retford Town, Gainsborough Trinity, and Chesterfield FC, in various guises, in numerous newspaper articles. This gives the club a claim on being the fourth oldest in the world.

Founding Fathers.

Football (a hybrid form of rugby and association football) was played at the Pestalozzian school Worksop in the 1840's. In 1844, a boy called Muspratt arrived at the school from Liverpool and his memoirs vividly emphasise the sporting opportunities available to the pupils, who included the sons of the Khedive of Egypt. The school was blessed with 20 acres of playing fields and a gymnasium.

The Pestalozzian School, Worksop, where football was being played from the 1840s (BM)

Whilst bad eyesight precluded him from playing cricket, Muspratt 'eagerly took part in football and other games.' The Pestalozzian team that played Worksop in 1873, winning by one goal to nil, had a continental flavour, with players such as Pignet, D'Auriol and Kraemer in the line-up.

A Victorian gentleman from Worksop played a significant role in developing the global game. Michael Ellison, land agent to the powerful Duke of Norfolk, helped form Sheffield Club. He was timekeeper for Sheffield Club and became Secretary. He built Bramall Lane, the oldest professional multi-purpose sports ground in the world, on the Duke of Norfolk's land in 1854. Ellison was the first President of Sheffield United and Yorkshire County Cricket Club.

Worksop's earliest footballers were 'gentlemen' from land-owning and professional classes. Solicitors, surgeons, and lawyers found time to pursue the new leisure pursuit of football. Prior to the establishment of a half-day holiday the working classes would generally only have time for football on holiday or feast days.

John Appleton, the son of the vicar of the historic Worksop Priory Church is the most likely founder of a recreational football club in Worksop in 1861, a club designed to keep cricketers and volunteer soldiers from the Worksop branch of the Robin Hood Rifles fit in the winter months. John Appleton was a solicitor who trained in Sheffield and represented Sheffield FC in 1861. His brother Charles Appleton, who played football as a boy at Rossall school, an independent boarding school on the Fylde coast in Lancashire, may also have played a part in the club's foundation.

Long before Tottenham Hotspur was an entity Worksop FC were experimenting with new tactical innovations. In a game against Shireoaks the *Sheffield Telegraph* reported, 'Pearson, working hard close in, passed to Mayor who neatly headed in through.'

Heading was a feature of the Sheffield game but a novelty in London. In Geoffrey Green's book, '*The World Game'* the author describes how, when Sheffield played London in 1875, the Sheffield players equally amused the press and spectators, by 'butting the ball with their heads.'

Worksop's early games were against clubs from the Sheffield area, although they did play against the Castle club of Nottingham. In the 1860s and 1870s the game was a robust affair, sometimes played on frozen pitches or in inches of snow. Hacking was commonly deployed in 'scrimmages' and games sometimes ended in 'free fights.' A Sheffield Telegraph report of a game between Worksop FC and Woodhouse Mill FC provides a cameo of a game in this era.

'During a fine scuffle, close to the boundary hedge, Pearson - a Worksop player - fairly impaled an opponent, giving him a back throw, which landed him on top of the hedge, where he hung quivering as in balance for some moments, amidst the shouts and cheers of the field.' Perhaps the first 'spear-tackle' ever recorded!

In the early years Worksop FC are reported as playing in green and white horizontal stripes, switching to plain dark blue around 1876. In the 1890's they changed again, sporting black and white halves or quarters, the racing colours of the Duke of Portland. They were known as 'the Donovans' in this era after a horse owned by the Duke of Portland that triumphed in the Derby and St Ledger. In 1894 they adopted a new kit of black and white stripes after Notts County became the first Nottinghamshire club to win the FA Cup.

The Worksop Town team that beat Rotherham Town in the FA Cup 1893-1894 (GB)

In 1898, when Nottingham Forest achieved the same feat, beating Derby County 4-1, Forest brought the FA Cup and their cup-winning team to Worksop. Inspired by this, Worksop switched to a red kit. This was the kit worn by the famous Arsenal and Huddersfield manager Herbert Chapman when he became a Worksop Town player in 1900. Coincidentally, Arsenal's choice of colours was inspired by a charitable donation from Forest in the same year.

Worksop remained in red shirts until, impressed by Nottinghamshire's County Cricket Championship win in the 1907 season, when peals of church bells rang out across the county in celebration, they switched to a green kit and became known as 'the Shamrocks.' The most important change came after post-war regeneration in 1919, when the club merged with Manton Colliery Athletic and were gifted shirts in the amber/yellow and black of the Manton Colliery club. Thus, even though they have occasionally flirted with other colour combinations, in living memory, Worksop Town FC have always been 'the Tigers.'

4. Tottenham Hotspur. A village in Middlesex.

Tottenham was once a separate entity from the City of London. Early settlements developed around the old Roman Road, known as Ermine Street, which evolved, in part, into the A10. It appears in the Domesday Book with 70 families living in association with the local manor.

The River Lea (or Lee) formed the eastern boundary between the municipal boroughs of Tottenham and Walthamstow, originally the ancient boundary between Middlesex and Essex. It also formed the western boundary of the Viking controlled Danelaw (Worksop was situated well within this area of Scandinavian jurisdiction). Today it is the boundary between the London boroughs of Haringey and Waltham Forest. A culverted river, the Moselle, a tributary of the Lea, crosses the borough from west to east.

The Moselle often caused serious flooding until it was mostly covered in the 19th century. In the Tudor era Henry VIII hunted in Tottenham woods. Like Worksop, Tottenham remained an attractive, aspirational semi-rural area. It was a settlement in Middlesex up to the 1860's, when the demographic began to change from middle to working class.

The latter decades of the 19th century brought rapid economic and social change. The arrival of the railway facilitated a mass building programme targeting the lower-middle and working-class ends of the market. The transformation was almost complete by the time Tottenham Hotspur Football Club were formed by a group of grammar school boys, learned enough to know about the characters in plays by William Shakespeare.

Harry Hotspur.

In 1882, should any of the Worksop gentlemen have picked up a broadsheet newspaper to peruse the progress of their beloved game in the capital (as we shall see, they may have been interested) the name of a new club, less dramatic than that of the East End club, Crouch End Vampires, but a curious combination, nevertheless, may have caught their eye. Tottenham Hotspur, formed by a group of schoolchildren and named after a Shakespeare character Harry Hotspur, had arrived, and were taking their first tentative steps on their path to glory. Two years later their fixture list was published in *The Tottenham Herald* for the first time, and, in the 1885/1886 season, they entered the London Association Cup. Just as Worksop Football Club had had a rude awakening when they first tested themselves against one of the Sheffield clubs, Hotspur would be thrashed 8-0 by the Casuals in the Second Round.

The first sign that a mighty oak might grow from the Tottenham acorn came a year later. On November 19th 1887, they played a club called Royal Arsenal and after the latter scored what *The Tottenham and Edmonton Herald* described as 'a lucky goal' the Tottenham men took control of the game. They were leading 2-1 when the contest was abandoned due to bad light. In the era of amateurism and friendly fixtures such decisions were far from uncommon, playing the game in the right spirit occasionally took precedence over the pursuit of victory.

In London, as the 1894/95 season commenced, the Tottenham Hotspur football team were considering embracing professionalism. The potential of a club with a huge population on its doorstep was becoming apparent after a breakthrough on the pitch. Tottenham had their first English cup run of note, beating West Herts, Wolverton and Clapton. In the 4th Qualifying Round they faced the first London team to embrace professionalism, paying players by 1890 and turning fully professional a year later. Spurs had the opportunity to listen, watch and learn as they earned a replay before losing 4-0 to Fulham.

5.   A Modern World.

From our perspective, aspects of daily life in the 1920s can appear to be primitive. In the mining village of Shireoaks, less than two miles from Worksop, there was coal to burn to heat the houses, but water was still being collected from 'tubs' positioned in the communal yards to collect rainwater. Poverty was endemic and lives were cut short by epidemics of tuberculosis, smallpox , pneumonia, and many other infectious diseases.

Beloved and Betrayed

Miners cottages, 'Tub Row', Shireoaks 1920s (IC)

However, people living in the 'Roaring Twenties' compared their lives to those of their parents and grandparents. Many felt blessed to be living in a 'modern world' of incredible technological innovation, and liberation from the horrors of war. The Great War was frequently called the 'War to End All Wars' and millions believed that a new era of permanent peace and prosperity was emerging from the global trauma of 1914/18.

The twenties was a decade when social life was dominated by the cinema, wireless, fashion and dance. The decade of the Charleston, Fox Trot and Tango. People flocked to amateur and professional sports arenas in huge numbers and the working classes discovered the benefits of country hiking for the first time.

The men who had survived the war had expectations of the peace and were more willing to challenge authority. 700 Worksop soldiers expressed their disapproval of government plans to send a captured German machine gun and other souvenirs of the war to Worksop (they also expressed a desire to forget the horror they had experienced) and a deputation of Worksop Town players met club officials, President

Longbottom and Chairman Tomlinson to demand a new era of industrial relations.

The group was mostly composed of veteran pre-war players like Bert Floyd, Levi Copestake and George Blackburn, but also included a self-confident and opinionated youngster called Tommy Lawrie who had yet to establish himself in the first-team. Together they demanded a club 'fit for heroes,' work-free match days (with expenses paid), compensation for any loss of earnings sustained and a reduction in the number of officials travelling free of charge to away games. Most of their demands would be implemented by the middle of the next decade, the latter being a notable exception, but only young Lawrie would survive in the first-team squad long enough to appreciate their success.

Alderman Charles Arthur Longbottom (1864/1935).

Noted for being the first Mayor of Worksop and first Freeman of the Borough in addition to his extensive business and mining interests, Charles Longbottom was popularly known as 'Charley' by the Worksop Town supporters. Although he had been on the football club's board of directors in the pre-war period, and had saved the club from financial meltdown, it was in the post-war period that his investment came to fruition. He was to be the driving force behind Worksop's regeneration, and he was the principal benefactor behind the club's cup and league success.

Originally Longbottom was a civil engineer, before joining his father's business as a colliery agent, eventually building up the business of Longbottom and Company, Coal Distributors. Longbottom & Co. became a well-known and well-established Sheffield company the early to mid-20th century. The company bought and transported vast quantities of coal, some 15,000 tonnes per month, mainly from New Hucknall Colliery and Shireoaks Colliery. It was a lucrative enterprise and Longbottom was soon a very wealthy man.

A man of extensive business interests, Longbottom also became director of Swann, Ratcliffe and Co. (silica brick manufacturers), of Steel and Garland Ltd. (iron founders), General Timber Supplies Ltd., Oates Ltd. (timber merchants and handle manufacturers), the Newfoundland and St. Lawrence Timber Supplies Ltd. and of Delaney, Ltd.

In a move that was mutually advantageous to all parties, he became a director of the Shireoaks Colliery Company, Worksop, in the early 1920s. By 1925 he had become chairman, by which time the company's five collieries were regularly outputting 1,000,000 tons per year.

Also of some significance, in 1913, was his appointment as President of Worksop Town Football Club, triggering an ambitious plan to raise finance, recruit quality players and transform the Midlands League side into a Football League club.

Longbottom lived at Forest Hill House, Worksop. His personal worth at his death in 1935 was £128,000 – an equivalent of around £9.75 million today.

6. Worksop Town. Midland League Champions.
The power of Wireless and Looping the Loop.

Worksop Town were quick to embrace the exciting new technological innovations of the decade. A huge boom in post-war crowds, the generosity of their wealthy benefactor Charles Longbottom and a thriving supporters club, all conspired to drive a push for Midland League success, FA Cup glory and Football League status. They were soon to experience an era of sustained excellence.

At the AGM in July 1921, the club was in credit (a rare occurrence during Worksop Town's chequered history.) The positive balance of £54 12s and 3p, £2,615 in today's money, facilitated drainage of the notorious Central Avenue quagmire. Crowds swiftly raced to a 3,000 average, with over 7,000 attending important games.

From footballs, coloured in amber and black, delivered to the centre spot by a cheery pilot looping the loop, (against Nelson) to a radio attached to the main stand roof broadcasting live commentary of the 1927 FA Cup Final between Cardiff and Arsenal, in this era Worksop were an ambitious, go-ahead club. In April 1922, Chairman Longbottom would finally see some return for bankrolling the club for many years.

The 1921/22 campaign opened auspiciously away from home. A good following made the journey to the pretty spa-town of Harrogate to see the local heroes face Harrogate FC for the first time. A 3-1 victory was a statement of intent by the Tigers.

Supporters began to sense that this might be a special season for Worksop Town when they travelled to Hillsborough to play against Wednesday Reserves on October 15th 1921. Games against the talented reserve sides of the two Sheffield clubs provided the best indications of capability for serious title contenders. A huge following from Worksop cherished a 1-0 victory, Charlesworth scoring the winner from a Huxford cross. It was a triumph that alerted the premier teams in south Yorkshire and the north Midlands to the potential of Worksop Town.

In November, as the German mark crumbled and the country descended into anarchic turmoil, Worksop's footballing credit was on the rise. A crowd of over 3,000 saw Town entertain Nottingham Forest Reserves at a freshly painted and pristine Central Avenue. A brace from Lawrie secured a 2-0 win, an embarrassment to the Nottingham professionals, scarcely reflecting the superiority of the Tigers.

Worksop were now top of the league for the first time, crowds of over 3,000 were the norm and the club was the talk of the town. Worksop Town's football programmes in this era reflect a sense of professional competence and stability, for the first time they contained photographs and information on where to indulge in the best pre-and post-match food and entertainment. The new Co-operative Restaurant, Short's Yankee Bar, and the Waverley Hotel were amongst the most favoured establishments.

A 2-1 FA Cup victory against a Nelson team containing three full internationals, who were good enough to beat Real Madrid in a pre-season friendly and achieve promotion to the Second Division in the following season, was a statement of intent. The victory, in front of 5,030 at Central Avenue, wetted appetites. The Nelson leader lamented that the Lancastrians were 'overwhelmed in a whirlwind start' noting the intensity and the 'war-cries' of the Worksop support.

Only a myopic referee and linesman saved a fortunate Southend United side from defeat at Central Avenue in the next round (a disallowed Worksop goal was seen to roll down the inside of the net before being cleared). An impressive crowd of 6,614 went home convinced of the Tigers' championship and Football League potential.

A game against Scunthorpe United in January loomed large as a decisive moment in the campaign. With outbreaks of foot and mouth and typhoid fever reported across the country and fog a local hazard, Worksop's much lauded unbeaten home record was under threat from 'the Nuts,' as Scunthorpe were then called. Scunthorpe, the most in-form team in the Midland League, had won nine successive games.

A crowd approaching 3,500 saw a pulsating contest on a snow-covered ground. Worksop attacked from the start and scored twice in the opening ten minutes, Tommy Lawrie, always a man for the big occasion, opened their account and Richardson added a penalty. When Banks added a third shortly after the re-start the excited home fans celebrated an inevitable home victory. United had other ideas, however, scoring two swift goals in reply. Even when Lilley scored with a superb strike to put Town further ahead Scunthorpe replied. The Tigers hung on, however, winning 4-3 and edging closer to a first league title.

Mansfield Again. A Nottinghamshire Derby.

Destiny decreed that Worksop's visitors for the defining game of the season would be Mansfield Town. A rivalry from the previous century that had lain dormant for decades was thriving again, as the Tigers were poised, just one point away from the glory of a first ever Midland League title. Excitement had been growing during the final weeks of the season. The momentum increased with success over the Easter period, and a crowd of 4,500, with 1,000 travelling from Mansfield and affiliated villages, by train, car and on foot, gathered to see the drama unfold.

Mansfield won the toss and kicked off with the sun behind them and a stiffening wind in their favour. However, it was Worksop who created the early chances. The normally reliable Bert Lilley missed a couple of open goals to the evident frustration of the expectant home support. Mansfield had chances too, but Jack Brown was outstanding in goal until a long shot from Sheldon swerved and dipped, completely deceiving him, giving Mansfield a one-goal advantage. Worksop's momentum stalled and their usually fluent passing game broke down.

There was huge relief when the Tigers were awarded a penalty, but the normally deadly specialist, Tom Richardson, missed in front of the Canal End. Just when it seemed that it was not going to be the Tiger's day, Wilf Simmonite popped up with a critical goal and the home support erupted in delight. Although there were chances at either end the scores remained even.

As a Mr Joseph Stalin was appointed General Secretary of the Communist Party and a wireless cable was activated between Egypt and England, the world's fourth oldest football club were declared Champions of the Midland League for the first time.

As champions, the Tigers would have the honour of hosting The Rest of the League XI on Thursday, April 27th 1922. It was a moment long overdue, but there could be no doubt that Worksop were worthy champions of a league that still contained the reserve teams of some of the most powerful clubs in the land, as well as the representative sides of towns significantly bigger than Worksop.

7. October 1922. Worksop's FA Cup Campaign

Fourth Qualifying Round. Scunthorpe United. Home.

In the Cup, Worksop entered at the Fourth Qualifying Round, the Tigers being exempt up to this stage after success in the previous two seasons. In this era, the First Division clubs entered at the First Round stage, the equivalent of the Third Round today.

When the ambitious Lincolnshire side, Scunthorpe United arrived in town to contest the tie, around, 3,350 fans descended on Central Avenue. 60 Scunthorpe fans came on a special train from Frodingham, others by road. Worksop fans with main stand seating tickets, were given the opportunity to book their own seats in advance, a novelty at that time.

Scunthorpe had progressed impressively with qualifying wins at Gainsborough and Boston in the Second and Third Rounds, and, from the start, the game was played at a punishing pace. The Tigers produced some excellent football in a pulsating FA Cup encounter against an aggressive and attack-minded visiting eleven, the first five goals being scored in 20 minutes of end-to-end football. Cawley scored a brace-both perfectly placed rather than struck - and Lawrie added another, 'a rattling good header' in his own words, to give the Tigers a 3-2 half-time lead.

The contest settled down after half-time, but Worksop continued to pass and move efficiently. The final strike was the pick of the goals, a spectacular shot from Wally Amos. It cannoned into the net off the foot of a Scunthorpe player, Amos suggesting that both players made contact at the same time.

Fifth Qualifying Round. Grimsby Town. Away.

With the news that Grimsby Town would face the Tigers at home in the next round of the FA Cup, *The Hull Daily Mail* immediately began speculating on the outcome of a Hull v Grimsby clash, after Worksop had been dismissed from the competition. It announced that everyone outside of Worksop would 'rightly expect a victory for the Mariners.' The club and the Grimsby sports reporters appeared to have forgotten the previous FA Cup clash of 1894, when Worksop, who were then close to the bottom of the Sheffield Association League, caused a sensational upset by defeating Grimsby, who were riding high, third-placed in the Second Division.

The Mariners were now a mid-table side in the Third Division North, a league currently being dominated by Nelson, the Lancashire side defeated comfortably by the Tigers in the FA Cup the season before. It was this result that inspired self-belief in the ranks of the Worksop players. Even without home advantage Worksop were quietly confident that history could be repeated.

The light was poor as play commenced and conditions worsened as a sea fret drifted over the ground. Grimsby strived to sink the part-timer's challenge swiftly. Graver's shot skimmed the bar and Bratley headed out Coupland's shot which looked to be heading for the Worksop goal as the Mariners pressed. Backed by a vociferous army of travelling supporters, the Tigers dug-deep, determined to force a draw and gain a home replay. As Grimsby stormed forward the ball burst with an audible 'plop' which startled the crowd and stalled the early momentum of the home side. Worksop were resisting the Grimsby attacks with typical resilience and the home crowd soon became frustrated and restless.

Grimsby's attacks were easily repulsed, and the Lincolnshire men became ill-disciplined as their initial attacking forays were thwarted. The Mariners supporters became subdued and worried, and surprised by the defensive competence and self-confidence of the Worksop team. The

Tigers began to counter, building swiftly from the back with neat passing combinations. Spink forced the first save from Harrison, the Grimsby custodian.

As the Worksop's players sensed their opponent's unease, they started to create more chances. A smart interchange between Spink and Lilley, the latter set up with a perfectly timed pass, brought the first critical moment of the game. The man who had survived a gassing in the trenches took his first opportunity with typical nonchalance.

In the second half, the Mariners started brightly, creating a chance for Graver. His fine strike was saved by Jack Brown at full stretch, and Worksop looked to counter swiftly.

Lawrie left the Grimsby defender, Miller 'looking like a stuffed dummy' according to *The Worksop Guardian* reporter as he dribbled past him comfortably to start the move. His goal was an old-school classic, Spinks's cross, Lawrie's one touch with his right foot and a familiar bulge in the back of the net. There was no way back for the thoroughly disheartened Third Division North side.

For Grimsby, as *The Derby Telegraph* pointed out, defeat was a 'bitter pill to swallow' after their display of pre-match arrogance. The local press ruefully reflected on the worst FA Cup performance for 25 years and a shock defeat to 'a team reputedly of inferior class.'

Sixth Qualifying Round. Chesterfield. Home.

A home draw in the sixth, and final qualifying round, against local rivals Chesterfield, was a tremendous reward. Chesterfield despite being a larger town, boasting a significant population advantage over their Notts rivals, had often been outfought, and defeated, on visits to Worksop. They had visited Worksop's Central Avenue ground on eight occasions in the Midland League, obtaining a solitary point in 1912/13 to punctuate seven straight defeats. In the 1914/15 season Chesterfield had been beaten 7-0. The solitary 'Spireite' success had come in the Midland Combination in 1915/16. This would be the first FA Cup clash between the two towns, and the first occasion when Chesterfield would be facing the Tigers as a Football League club. A victory for the Spireites, despite their advanced status, was far from guaranteed.

Charles Longbottom, President of Worksop Town Football Club circa 1923 (TC)

There was a commendable aura of professional competence associated with the Worksop club's match-day organisation in this era, from pre-match lunch stops before away games, to advice for players on training methods when recovering from injury. Even the self-promotion was astute. In 1923 the club billed themselves as 'the small-town club with a big heart.' It was a slogan that reflected both the affection felt by the townsfolk for the club, and the fighting spirit of the footballers drawn from the collieries.

Beloved and Betrayed

Bridge Street looking south showing the Gaiety Picturedome and the Waverley Hotel 1920s (IC)

Prior to the Chesterfield game players were instructed to attend the Waverley Hotel, a grand name for the Bridge Street Café, at 11:30 for lunch.

Central Avenue sold out swiftly for this encounter, season ticket holders were reminded of the need to show their cards on arrival. The Tigers made only one change from the team that had defeated the Mariners, Cawley an experienced professional who had played for both Leeds United and the Wednesday, replacing the unlucky veteran Lilley. The line-up for this memorable clash was: Brown, Bratley, Richardson, Simmonite, Robinson, Froggatt, Amos, Cawley, Rippon, Lawrie and Spink. In retrospect, one of the best teams ever to wear the amber and black of Worksop Town.

Two special trains were deployed by the Great Central Railway Company to bring a sizeable contingent of enthusiastic Spireite fans into town. With old rivals Mansfield also making the FA Cup Final Qualifying Round, interest in the English Cup was intense across the whole region. The Derbyshire papers and *The Worksop Guardian* both speculated on the psychological impact of Chesterfield's dismal record at

Worksop. Whilst it was acknowledged that the Third Division side should be classed as favourites against a non-league side, the visiting supporters were clearly anxious.

On a typical Central Avenue surface, heavy in some areas and slippery in others, the Tigers adapted quickly and appeared to be psychologically better prepared. They were quicker on the ball and their tackling was more aggressive and tenacious. They preyed on the Chesterfield goal, with long sweeping passes often finding their target, as the home fans began to sense an upset.

In contrast, Chesterfield struggled to get sustained spells of possession, their best players looked nervous on the ball as if too anxious to take any risks. The classic ingredients of an upset were in place.

When Saxby, the Chesterfield defender, was pressed hard, he panicked, kicking the ball desperately against Rippon. He could only watch as it cannoned off towards the left, straight to the feet of the Tiger's winger.

A perfect cross was met by Tommy Lawrie, who crashed the ball in off the post. It was no fluke. Worksop were playing the better football. Brown had only one save to make in the first half. He was as alert as ever, tipping Garrett's shot around the post.

In the second half, Chesterfield made a desperate fight of a game that was rapidly slipping away. Although the Spireites dominated possession in the middle of the pitch, the Tigers fought tenaciously in the final third and Chesterfield created little. Fifteen minutes into the second period Leddy made a hapless challenge on Amos - it was a clear penalty.

Amidst scenes of incredible excitement and tension, Worksop's skipper Richardson stepped forward. Could he put the game out of reach? His shot was on target, but keeper Hibberd saved and managed to fall on the ball. As players from both sides rushed in, something approaching a hybrid of old-fashioned hacking scrimmage and a general mêlée ensued. For a time, it looked as if the referee would have to take drastic action and send several players off before order was restored.

For the remainder of the game, the Tigers defended heroically. Brown made many fine saves and the swift counter-attacks led by Lawrie, Spink, Amos and Rippon provided a much-needed respite. As the clock moved on, the crowd counted down and the game concluded with a roar that could be heard in the surrounding villages. The crowd of 7,373 was a new record for the ground, as were the receipts of just over £408. *The Worksop Guardian* headline blazed the glorious news, 'Blues dismissed. Another Third Division team defeated.'

Mixed Reactions.

When the draw for the First Round was made on Monday, December 18th 1922, there was a euphoric response across the whole town to the news that the Tigers would visit London to face the mighty Tottenham Hotspur, already established as one of the most glamorous and successful clubs in the world, and one of the favourites to grace the first FA Cup Final at the new £750,000 Wembley Empire Stadium.

In Tottenham, the response to the draw was one of quiet, smug satisfaction. Once again Dame Fortune had smiled on God's chosen team. They had the easiest draw against the weakest team still left in the competition. The result was a formality and the dream of appearing at the first Cup-Final to be played at London's remarkable new stadium had moved appreciably closer. Scarcely any Spurs supporters had heard of Worksop, and the ones who had, were dismissive. *The Daily Mail* described 'colliery men' from 'an untidy coal-smoked little town' predicting 'a slaughter of innocents.'

8.   Chelsea.

The delight at being drawn against one of the world's elite footballing institutions was not a completely new experience for Worksop Town's older supporters. In 1908, a very ordinary Worksop side had a fortuitous run of draws, including a bye in the Final Qualifying Round and found themselves in the hat for the First Round of the FA Cup.

There was unprecedented excitement in the town when the club's supporters discovered that they had been drawn to play at home against Chelsea. Chelsea were already a huge club, playing in front of crowds up to 60,000 at their Stamford Bridge home and Worksop's directors agreed to switch the tie for financial gain. It was a rational, calculated, and understandable decision but it broke the hearts of supporters who could not afford the trip to London.

Beloved and Betrayed

It made the result a foregone conclusion and eroded some of the magic from the FA Cup experience for fans and players alike, although the players made the best of it. Common sense suggested that the serious challenge of bridging the gap between the Midland League, and the top tier of English football would be practically impossible without home advantage.

In their last Midland League game prior to facing the famous London side, Town defeated Mexborough by a record margin of 6-1 when most supporters assumed that they would be taking it easy on a frozen pitch.

Captain Richardson was quoted speaking confidently, if colloquially, in *The Sheffield Daily Telegraph* - 'It's too much like braggin' to say we shall beat em on their own bit of turf, but they'll hev to keep hoppin' around to keep our little uns out.'

Mr F Newnes the MP for Bassetlaw who had a printing business in the capital, invited the team, officials and the committee to dine with him after the game, a splendid entertainment being prepared by the genial local MP.

The Great Northern announced that they were running a special to bring the fans down. As anticipation and excitement grew, the 'probables' and 'possibles' had a combined practice match to give the 'possibles' a chance to force their way into the First XI. The selected Worksop Town players were then informed that they would leave on Friday and set up base in the Imperial Hotel, Russell Square.

The papers generally put an upbeat spin on the decision to switch the tie and *The Worksop Guardian* in particular, supported the directors wholeheartedly in their decision - but many of the faithful 'day in day out, all weather' supporters were dismayed.

The game was, as most realists anticipated, a one-sided affair, the 9-1 score-line reflecting the anticipated and inevitable dominance of the white-shirted London team on their own ground. Worksop were delighted with the support they received from the Chelsea fans who appreciated their bravery, if not their skill. Their solitary goal, secured by George Richardson, brought the biggest cheer of the day.

The generosity of Mr F Newnes was not in doubt and the Gaiety Restaurant in the Strand put on a spectacular treat for the Worksop and

Chelsea guests. Facing each other at the end of the dining table were two goals in the Shamrock Green of Worksop and suspended from them were ten balls to represent the number of goals scored in the match, five on each goal so as not to upset the sensibilities of the defeated Town players. A sculpture of a footballer cut from a solid block of ice crowned the pudding.

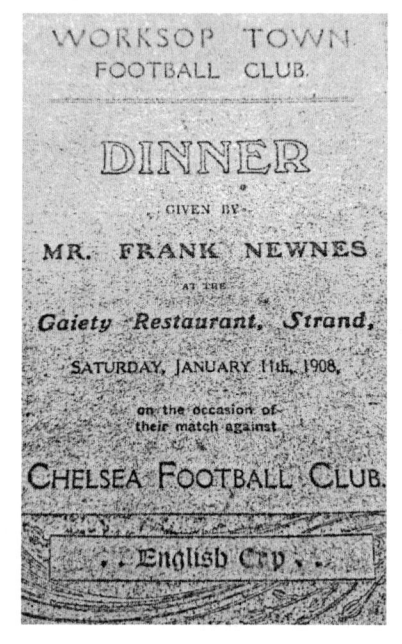

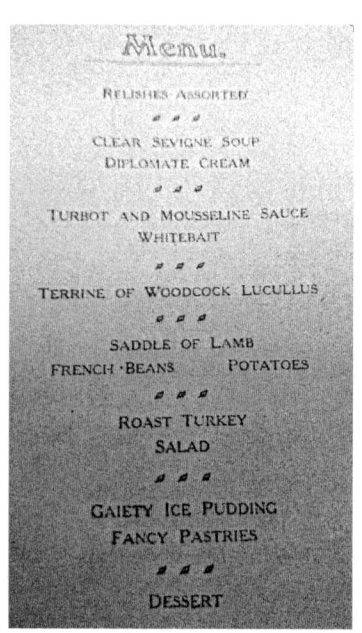

WORKSOP TOWN FOOTBALL CLUB.

DINNER

GIVEN BY:

MR. FRANK NEWNES

AT THE

Gaiety Restaurant, Strand,

SATURDAY, JANUARY 11th, 1908,

on the occasion of
their match against

CHELSEA FOOTBALL CLUB.

English Cup.

Menu.

RELISHES ASSORTED

CLEAR SEVIGNE SOUP
DIPLOMATE CREAM

TURBOT AND MOUSSELINE SAUCE
WHITEBAIT

TERRINE OF WOODCOCK LUCULLUS

SADDLE OF LAMB
FRENCH BEANS   POTATOES

ROAST TURKEY
SALAD

GAIETY ICE PUDDING
FANCY PASTRIES

DESSERT

Post-match banquet at the Gaiety Restaurant, Strand (FN)

At the top of the table was chairman AJ Tomlinson, a man destined to still be in post fifteen years later. Alongside him was Mr EG Warburton, a board member, and a local solicitor, Mr Stephen Box. The chairman of the local council and Mr J Blundell the secretary, were also honoured guests.

Amongst the guests invited from London was Mr HW Hewitt of the famous Corinthians club. In all, over 100 guests were invited to attend. They included A Watson of Mansfield who had played with Worksop and then with Notts County when they won the Cup, and E Allsopp who was a star of the first Worksop team to enter the FA Cup some 18 years earlier.

In the aftermath of the game the scale of the defeat added to the sense of deflation and to the general feeling of disappointment at the director's decision. The chairman AJ Tomlinson was said to have promised that, if the opportunity arose to bring a top club to Worksop again, they would seize it.

Gateford Road, Worksop 1908 (IC)

9. Goliath v David

'The past is another country, they do things differently there.'
LP Hartley.

After achieving arguably the greatest giant-killing feat of all time when they became the first and only non-league side to win the FA Cup in 1901, Spurs should perhaps have shown a little more deference to the magical uncertainty of a competition which, despite a steady erosion of credibility, can still stir the imagination and thrill the grass roots football supporter like no other (as demonstrated during a remarkable Third Round in 2022, when Cambridge United, Kidderminster Harriers,

Nottingham Forest and others added another chapter to the rich history of the FA Cup).

However, in 1923, only a tiny part of the FA Cup story had been written, the feats of Walsall v Arsenal in 1933, (Herbert Chapman's last FA Cup tie), the drama of Yeovil's sloping pitch facilitating the defeat of Sunderland in 1949, Colchester United beating Leeds United at Layer Road in 1971 and perhaps the most famous upset of all time, the following season, when Hereford United defeated Newcastle United, were all decades away.

In January 1923, there was only a scattering of historic results that defied logic and put an element of doubt into the minds of habitually pessimistic supporters and, as we have seen, most Spurs fans were of the 'glass half full variety.'

Whilst Tottenham Hotspur's achievement in 1901, becoming the first, and almost certainly the only, non-league club to lift the FA Cup was remarkable, the Southern League was scarcely a haven for minnows. Whilst not on par with the First Division it could be classed as a parallel Second Division in terms of quality and the size of the towns in the cohort.

Many Southern League clubs were exempted from the Qualifying Stages of the FA Cup, and there were Football League clubs who did not benefit from exemption. It was not unusual therefore to see Southern League clubs challenging in the later stages of the country's most prestigious competition. Southampton reached two FA Cup Finals as a Southern League club, and the Southern League often featured at the quarter and semi-final stages.

The possibility that a team of Spurs stature could lose to a team from a place scarcely anyone had heard of, a community that was still, technically, a mining village, stretched imaginative capability to the limit. Spurs would win and score plenty of goals in so doing.

However, as we have seen, at this point in its history, Worksop Town had reached the moment when the slow evolution of a football culture, in a town that had been engaged with the game from its earliest days, had reached its zenith. In 1923 it was a club that oozed self-confidence and feared no one. It had been punching above its weight since the double victories over Leeds United in 1919 and had already knocked out three Football League clubs in a decade that was still in its infancy.

The victory over local rivals Chesterfield, the club that had outmanoeuvred Worksop Town in their campaign to be elected to the Third Division North, had cemented the love affair between Worksop and its football team. No Worksop team, before or since, inspired such devotion. They were indeed beloved.

A Small Town Team with a Big Heart.

The journey to White Hart Lane had been a team effort. The men, women and children who lived in the town knew that the nine miners who worked at the local collieries and cycled miles from the villages to train after working a full shift underground, or sat with their mates on public transport, were of their community. They metaphorically, and literally in some cases, shared their DNA.

Their success could be cherished because so many had played their part. Colleagues swapped shifts to enable players to travel to midweek games and replays. Dozens actively worked on their behalf, raising huge sums of money through the supporter's club.

The supporter's club was a finely tuned machine that was the envy of rival Midland League clubs. It had recently raised £750 to fully fund the building of new changing rooms. In 1921, when Mansfield Town wanted to start a supporter's club of their own, they had no hesitation in inviting the Worksop supporters committee to advise and inspire Mansfield supporters at their inaugural meeting. The wording on the caption on a picture in the professional programme produced weekly - 'Our Boys' - reflected the affection felt by the supporters to the young men representing the club and the town.

For the miners of Creswell, Kiveton, Manton, Shireoaks, Steetley, Whitwell and elsewhere, the nine Midland League first-teamers were also colleagues and comrades in arms. They shared the unique bonds of friendships forged in a working environment where trust was paramount, and men were judged on their technical understanding of the job at hand and their physical capability, rather than their social status.

Beloved and Betrayed

Old miners used to say that, when they were on holiday, they could spot a fellow miner by the shape of their body, and the way they walked. They were lean, muscular and powerful and carried themselves confidently. In his book *The Road to Wigan Pier,* George Orwell, reflecting on the toughness of the lives and the nature of their work wrote, 'If there is one man to whom I do feel myself inferior, it is a coal-miner.'

The cartoon carried by *The Daily Mail*, January 16th 1923, caricatured the Worksop players as gargantuan and physically intimidating, if clumsy. The cartoonist joked that they were 'missing their old pit mouth.' It was true that they were unlikely to be cowed or afraid by anyone they were likely to meet on a football field. Equally, more than any other representative of the working classes the coal-miner appreciated fresh air and exercise. Running around on a football field was always going to be a source of intense pleasure for men who had to routinely do seven hours (or more) of challenging, dirty, dangerous, invidious, back-breaking work underground.

The thriving Portland League had run out of appellations for local teams, Worksop United, Rovers, Athletic, Wanderers, North End, West End, Villa and Central all ran thriving senior and junior organisations, and the system that had produced Football League players on an industrial scale finally had a successful Midland League Club at the top of its pyramid. A worthy recipient of the best local talent.

Worksop also had another secret weapon. Trainer George Watkinson, affectionately known as 'Old George' had been around since the days when Herbert Chapman was playing for Worksop and offering opinions on tactics, training and strategy at the turn of the century. Watkinson possessed an experienced tactical brain and good contacts. He chose to spend Boxing Day 1922 at Bramall Lane, watching Tottenham lose 2-0 against Sheffield United, rather than travel with his well-drilled Midland League side to Gainsborough Trinity.

As we will discover, Watkinson was a man with a plan.

Worksop Town trainers 1923. T Slater and George Watkinson (TC)

Beloved and Betrayed

10. London Calling.

Tottenham Hotspur v Worksop Town. Saturday, January 13th 1923

This was Worksop Town's date with destiny, the game kicking off at 2.30pm, as was usual in the era before floodlights. The draw had already prompted discussion across the length and breadth of the land, the interest driven by the huge gulf in status, finance, and reputation between the two clubs. In the far north, *The Dundee Courier* suggested that Spurs would progress comfortably to the next round. *The Derby Daily Telegraph* cursed Spurs' 'proverbial good luck' and dismissed Worksop as, 'the easiest of things.'

Football had been in the news for the wrong reasons as the New Year dawned. A supporter in the north-east was pushed under a bus by hooligans and died because of his injuries. The judge described football fans in general as a 'disgrace to civilisation.' In happier news, the renowned walker, Tom Swift, announced that he was leaving Worksop market-place on the Sunday ahead of the fixture to walk to the Spurs game! This was not such an unusual feat. There was something of a tradition of supporters walking to FA Cup Finals, but Swift's progress would be followed avidly in Worksop.

As Worksop's directors prepared for the biggest game in the club's history, a special sub-committee was formed to deal with administration pertaining to the clash with Spurs. Mr Albert John Tomlinson, Frederick Hensley, and the secretary, George Storer were empowered to make all the critical decisions.

The financial committee met on January 1st, JW Caseldine, J Rawson and EG Rawson routinely approving a wage bill of £183.3.10 and expenses of £64.6.6 for payment. There is no suggestion in the minutes that the club were in dire financial straits.

The preparation was impressively professional in terms of attention to detail. The fifteen players selected for the London trip were instructed to report to Worksop's Central Avenue on Thursday, January 11th, for light training and baths! The team would be staying in one of London's best hotels, the Imperial in Russell Square (the same hotel they had stayed in prior to the Chelsea game) and the directors obviously wanted to leave the right kind of impression.

Tom Spink, one of a cluster of Worksop Town players who had played at a higher level was selected, despite medical advice suggesting that the infection on his knee, described as a boil or a carbuncle, would not heal in time. A meeting of the sub-committee was scheduled for late on Thursday evening to review the team, if required.

Then on January 9th Worksop's Cup hopes received a serious blow with the news that Spink, arguably Town's best player, would miss the tie. He was said to be 'devastated.'

On Thursday, January 11th, *The Nottingham Evening Post*, after providing an update on Tom Swift's progress – he'd passed through Northampton and was now at St Albans - announced that if the cup tie were to be replayed it would not be at Worksop but at one of the Sheffield grounds. It was a disclosure that appeared to have escaped the attention of the Worksop supporters.

Worksop had a formidable team by Midland League standards, Cawley and Lawrie both featured in that seasons league top-scoring charts with nine goals each, Spink and Brown were, without a doubt, a cut above non- league. However, nine of the team were engaged in the mines as late as Thursday and the Tigers were in the middle of an injury crisis, short of three first-team regulars, including their star forward and Vice-Captain.

Worksop's cup exploits had been national news in Victorian times, now, for probably the first time in their history, the Tigers went global. A crudely illustrated article in *The Rockford Times*, from Illinois USA, instructed its readers to think of Jack Brown as a 'human glider - leaping like a porpoise.' Soccer, it informed its American readers 'was like a cross between a rough rugby game and a trench raid.'

Living the Dream.

For the lads who had been working a full shift down the pit on the day before their London adventure, and for the directors, and the loyal supporters who could afford to make the trip, the forthcoming 48 hours would take on a dream-like quality. For many, it would be one of the most memorable experiences of their entire life - an adventure that they never tired of talking about.

The excitement began with the players being cheered off at Worksop station. The town band were in fine form playing rousing tunes. Affection for the players was palpable, as was the supporter's faith in their team. At Retford saloon cars were attached to the front of the train, and, shortly after the London Express had steamed out of Nottinghamshire, a five-course luncheon was served. Director Foster provided dessert. Around 400 spectators joined them on their adventure.

Most of the players were visiting the capital of the British Empire for the first time. Director Fred Hensley was assigned to the task of leading the party by London Underground and on foot. The players chatted excitedly as they strolled through the smoggy London streets, eventually arriving at the Imperial Hotel, Russell Square.

Hotel advertising circa 1923 (n/k)

Beloved and Betrayed

The Imperial Hotel, now demolished, was an identical twin of the hotel which still welcomes visitors from the north to this day, the Hotel Russell (notable in later years for hosting the banquet after England won the World Cup in 1966). The Imperial had 1,000 rooms, serviced by lifts. Hotel suites and elevators were both completely alien to young men familiar only with the terraced houses and back-to-backs of the north Midlands and the West Riding. From the start, the players joshed and joked, hid each other's shoes, and cracked lame jokes to disguise their unease and discomfort. They were instructed to 'do as they pleased' up to tea time.

The directors were following the template of the clubs' previous London adventure, the visit to Stamford Bridge to play Chelsea in 1908. On the night before the Spurs game, the players were taken to the Holborn Restaurant for tea, then to the London Palladium where they had reserved seats at the front to enjoy some of the theatrical superstars of the day, Charles Bignell, Marguerite Cornille, Tom Costello and Leo Dryden. This was followed by a light supper and an early night.

Some players could not sleep but stayed awake until the early hours, speculating about how it would feel to walk out onto the hallowed turf of White Hart Lane, to start as equals against legends of the English game, cup winners, and international household names. Would they be up to the job, or would they be humiliated as the Town team had been when they met the mighty Chelsea in 1908? They almost relished being just a bunch of part-timers, from a town somewhere in the north Midlands that no one had ever heard of, because they knew they were a good team. In their hearts they firmly believed that Spurs were in for a surprise.

Worksop's players and management were more cautious when delivering their pre-game thoughts than the 1908 Shamrocks had been, but it is still possible to detect an undertow of optimism from the people who knew the quality of the men at their disposal. Secretary George Storer talked of 'travelling to London to meet England's premier team' but he also dared to dream, suggesting, 'they might force a draw, who knows? Football is a funny old sport.'

As always things seemed different in the morning. The pranksters were out in force, swapping the boots that the lads had quaintly left outside their doors, too embarrassed to risk getting mud on the carpet. They fooled around, knocking on doors and larking about. One of the boys assigned to pass a message on to skipper Tom Richardson woke up an irate commercial traveller, several times, by mistake, bewildered by the long corridors.

Lest we Forget.

The mood changed again. The players had business to attend to, respects to be paid. Mr Tom Haydock, a local lad made good, 40 years a teacher and esteemed youth football coach in the capital, arrived to greet them and be their host. Tom had a motor charabanc which he was happy to put at the team's disposal. They travelled more somberly to Whitehall, to the Cenotaph, in Tom Haydock's car. A gift from a lady spectator, a huge Tiger, dressed in club colours was placed on the front seat.

At the Cenotaph the skipper, Richardson placed what *The Worksop Guardian* described as 'a beautiful floral tribute to the memory of fallen comrades Dick Slater and Wilf Bartrop.' The latter, one of Worksop's finest ever players, had won the FA Cup with Barnsley in 1912.

The players stood in silent tribute in front of a wreath in the Tigers 'colours and placed a card which read, 'In grateful and affectionate remembrance of all our old players and all other footballers who fell in the war.' It was a fine gesture which perhaps also helped to put the task at hand in perspective. Whilst it was a daunting task to face the firepower of the mighty Spurs, it was nothing to going over the top to be sprayed with bullets from Hiram Maxim's machine guns.

A 'Sing-Song' and a Lucky Mascot.

With the serious business over with, for now, there was another sea-change in the mood of the players as they pressed on with their great adventure, all muffled up against the chill January air. They laughed, joshed and teased each other as they rattled through the London fog, to meet their destiny. After a light lunch, they headed to White Hart Lane. On the final leg of their journey the players sang their favourite song, '*I Want Some Money*' - a jolly little tune (the music and lyrics are still available) and a hit of the day. The lyrics are particularly apt for a hungry Worksop Town team of any era, especially the chorus.

'*I want some money; Gimme some, Gimme some.*'

When the team arrived at the ground, they were greeted by supporters who were down for the cup. A lady supporter presented a second, even larger stuffed Tiger as a lucky mascot. Another presented Worksop's handsome dark haired skipper Tom Richardson with a lady's garter. The players were then filmed for a special production to be shown at Gaumont picture houses across the country.

'*Fight for the FA Cup First Round*' would be shown at the Gaiety Cinema in Worksop, for weeks after the game, and intermittently as late as the early 1960s. For now, the excitement of experiencing modern technology and the other distractions facilitated an upbeat mood.

'Nothing to lose. Everything to gain.'

As the players changed, still joking and fooling around to disguise their nerves, they were encouraged by Trainer, Watkinson and 'skipper' Richardson to reflect on what they had achieved so far. The scalps of two Football League clubs had been taken, one on their own patch. They had every right to feel confident in themselves and each other, and in the mantra of prospective giant-killers of any era, as Tommy Lawrie pointed out, they had nothing to lose and everything to gain.

The Spurs team were far from being arrogant 'big-time Charlies' - Jimmy Seed was not the only player sporting the famous white shirt who had been forced to overcome social disadvantage to achieve current pre-eminence, and they were aware that their success could still prove to be a fleeting aberration. One mis-timed tackle, or public humiliation, could end a career and send a First Division footballer tumbling back down the leagues, or even back to the factory floor.

Spurs had become the 'champions of the south' and the elite club in London by establishing a robust professional culture. The Worksop players noted their opponents' expressions of grim determination as they lined up, especially the frowning face of their captain Arthur Grimsdell. They would get no favours from Tottenham Hotspur; if they had the opportunity to wipe out the challenge of Worksop Town with a feast of goals, they would take it.

They were aware that Worksop were champions of the Midland League but saw no reason to check the Worksop Town team sheet. Spurs were assured and focused, knowing that if they maintained their standards there could only be one winner. The Londoners were determined to be the first team to lift the FA Cup at the magnificent new Wembley stadium, as such, Worksop at home in the First Round FA Cup tie was a small stepping stone to this objective.

This was no ordinary Worksop Town team. Although weakened by injuries it was the best squad of players in the club's history, and they had a few men, who, if their lives had taken a different path might have been capable of wearing the shirt with the cockerel motif themselves. The stand out examples were: future international Jack Brown, George Robinson, a solid and capable centre half, who, during the Great War, had represented the British Army Team against the Irish Army in Dublin and Wally Amos, a tricky and diminutive winger, destined to torment a Spurs defence and other top flight full-backs a few years later.

Worksop Town were champions of the Midland League in 1922, a league that contained the reserve teams of some of the strongest teams in the country. Both Sheffield clubs won major honours in this decade. Worksop had to face international players returning from injury and young men on the brink of extremely successful careers. Without the capability to display acute tactical awareness, and most critically, to have the flexibility to change their formation on the pitch, they would not have been able to achieve this feat.

Reports suggest Worksop Town had surprisingly sophisticated positional flexibility for a non-league side. In a Midland League game against Denaby United, full back Bratley makes a goal-line clearance but also hits a tremendous drive over the bar. In the same game George Robinson is praised for his defensive tackles but also lauded for having more shots on goal than the forwards. During the club's Midland League Championship season, George Robinson scored six goals, with full back, Tom Richardson adding eight from penalties and free kicks.

After a 3-0 victory over a strong Wednesday Reserve side, reporters noted Worksop's successful application of a counter attacking style. On January 15th 1921, *The Green 'Un* reflected on how it was common to see ex-Worksop players, such as Ted 'Raz' Linley, who made over 100 first class appearances for Birmingham City, still attending Worksop training sessions after their transfer.

Tottenham were about to be surprised by a team which lined up in a traditional formation but then then switched to WM. It was this deployment of the latest, cutting-edge innovation that gave them a platform to confound both the Spurs players, the national press, and the massed ranks of photographers camped behind the Worksop goal.

11. Tom Richardson and his Merry Men.

In his book *'Association Football and How to Play it'*, written in 1908, Spurs legend John Cameron, the man who played such a crucial role as player and manager in Tottenham's rise, made an astute observation about the last line of defence.

'Goalkeepers, like poets, are born, not made.'

He went on to give a template for the ideal custodian.

'My ideal for that position would be a man who stood six feet and weighed at least 13 stone, with an eye as keen as that of a hawk. He must be able to divine where and when the opposing forward is about to shoot. All the great goalkeepers have been of a fearless disposition, practically throwing themselves at the ball, even at the risk of receiving a kick from the attacking forward. Fearlessness is undoubtedly a tremendous asset in the making of a great goalkeeper. He must also have a perfect understanding with his backs, and they must trust him infinitely, which makes his responsibility all the greater.'

John Henry aka 'Jack' Brown was born on March 19th 1899, in Hodthorpe, a hamlet close to the village of Whitwell, built by the Shireoaks Colliery Company to house its workers at the newly opened Whitwell Colliery.

The Derbyshire village of Whitwell must have a claim on having produced more top sporting professionals than any village in England, perhaps the most famous being the snooker star, Joe Davis, world snooker and billiards champion from the 1920s to the 1940s. His Whitwell home, on Welbeck Street, has a heritage plaque commemorating him.

His brother, the genial, popular television-friendly, Fred Davis OBE (August 14th 1913 – April 16th 1998) was another outstanding Whitwell born professional player of snooker and English billiards. Fred Davis was World Snooker Champion from 1948 to 1956, and a two-time winner of the World Billiards Championship.

The Whitwell bothers were the only two players to win both snooker and English billiards world championships, and Fred is second on the list of those holding most world snooker championship titles, behind Joe.

Les Jackson, an outstanding England cricketer and Wisden Cricketer of the Year in 1959, played for Whitwell Cricket Club.

Harry Lowe, Liverpool's captain from 1913 to 1915, was an inspirational role model for the young Jack Brown who, as a boy, dreamed of scoring goals, rather than saving them. Known as 'Captain Courageous, ' Lowe was a natural leader. Having featured both at left- and right-half he moved into the centre of defence, playing as 'pivot' as it was called, in 1913/14. He was unfortunately injured in the penultimate League fixture and subsequently missed his club's first-ever appearance in an FA Cup Final, in 1914.

Other sporting stars from the village include Chris Adams, the Sussex and England cricketer and Ian Bennett, a professional goalkeeper.

Whitwell is only a brisk walk away from Worksop and Brown's birth was registered in Worksop. By June 1899, John was described as the youngest of four children to George and Minnie, living in Hodthorpe, Whitwell.. His father was a self-employed bricklayer.

By 1911 the family had moved to Worksop itself. John Henry was living with a younger sister and an older brother, and their parents, at 9 Dennis Street. His father was still laying bricks. Standing five feet, ten and a quarter and weighing 12 stone, seven and a half pounds, Brown did not quite fit Cameron's ideal template in size and weight, but Brown was certainly of fearless disposition, regularly injuring himself diving at the feet of opposition strikers.

Brown started his career as a junior centre-forward when he played for local clubs Worksop Wesley FC and Netherton FC. An astute coach at the latter noted Brown's prowess as a goal keeper in a training session and persuaded a reluctant Brown to make the switch. It was in this position that he came to the attention of Worksop Town, who moved swiftly to secure his services for the Tigers in 1919.

Beloved and Betrayed

When interviewed by a *Sunday Illustrated* reporter (Sunday January 21st 1923), Brown, who could leap like a salmon, kept his feet firmly on the ground.

'Football is all right as a weekend recreation, but it is sometimes as risky as mining.' Brown went on to illustrate the perils involved with a description of a boot stud splitting his nostril as he dived, with typical bravery at the feet of an opposing striker. Brown was also not immune to the eccentricities of his profession. He fastidiously stuck to wearing a brown top. Brown by name, Brown by jersey.

He was a strong willed and determined man who did not suffer fools gladly and sometimes challenged authority. In his early days at Worksop, he chose to go on holiday rather than play in a reserve-team fixture at Kiveton Park. Years later, his international career stalled after an altercation with a selector on a return ferry from Ireland.

Jack Brown circa 1923 (TC)

Full-Backs.

Left-Back, Tom Richardson, team captain since September 22nd 1919, stands out on team photographs. Broad shouldered and confident, he looks like a leader of men. Another Worksop man who took enormous pleasure from representing his home town club, he was a hero to the legions of small boys who gathered to watch the players train.

Richardson's nickname, 'Needham,' was so ubiquitous, so routinely used by colleagues, that visiting journalists sometimes recorded him as 'Tom Needham' in match reports. As a youngster he probably made a mistake in joining Sheffield United, a club that, at the time, boasted one of the most talented squads of professional footballers in the country. As with

Jimmy Seed at Sunderland, it was an onerous task for a young man to challenge for a first-team position. However, he did benefit from the coaching of Ernest Needham.

Herbert Chapman's favourite player, Needham was an exceptional footballer and a two-time FA Cup winning captain (1899 and 1902). He also captained United to their only league championship (1898). Such is his legacy that anyone who carries the surname Needham in Sheffield is automatically given the nickname 'Nudger' - an apt tribute to the player who ranks, statistically, as the greatest player in the club's history, and to the mastery of his short passing game.

In football there is rarely anything completely new under the sun and in Brian Judson's Spurs Odyssey website, the author includes a quotation from Arthur Rowe, the manager credited with the 'Push and Run' innovation that enabled the initial Tottenham Hotspur First Division Championship (1950/51). It could be straight from the 'Nudger' Needham coaching manual.

'I took our style back to the streets, the way we played it as kids - off the kerb, off the wall, taking the ball at different angles - enlisting the kerb as a teammate who let you have the ball back immediately after you had played it quickly .... the quicker the better. And all the time you were tailoring your ideas, your hopes to the limits or the limitations of your players, not asking them to do the things they could not do.'

Needham played 16 games for England and captained his country. Although nick-named for his short, punchy passing game, Needham's long passing game was so exceptional that Blades fans would have to wait until the era of Tony Currie in the 1960s and 1970s to see it's like again.

Writer Alfred Gibson wrote of Ernest Needham in 1906, 'This is one of the secrets of his greatness for very seldom when he has the ball is he deprived of it, whilst the accuracy of his wing passes, and the telling force of his punches straight across the field to an unprotected wing, spell danger to any kind of defence.'

As Spurs, and Fanny Walden in particular, would discover, Richardson, whilst not in the same league as the 'Prince of Half-Backs', had learnt a trick or two from Needham. He gave Tom the self-belief that enabled him to be fearless in his approach to facing any opponent regardless of their reputation, knowing that he had the timing and the balance required to compete at the highest level.

His son said that Tom was proud of being made captain of Sheffield United reserves and added that his father 'played five games for the first-team and was unbeaten in all of them.'

Tom Richardson joined the British Army in World War One. He was badly gassed at Cambrai but returned rapidly to the front, claiming to feel no ill effects. On his return to the battlefield, he was shot in the leg.

Alongside Richardson was another robust and uncompromising figure. Signed from Rotherham County in August 1921, Horace Bratley was from a locally famous Rawmarsh sporting family. His brother, Phillip, was the most famous member of the Bratley clan, one of the Barnsley team that won the 1912 FA Cup, playing in both the drawn first game, and the subsequent 1-0 replay victory over West Bromwich Albion (alongside Worksop's Wilf Bartrop).

Horace, whilst not as successful as his brother, was still a formidable defender. Stocky and pugnacious, he was known for the precision timing of his last-ditch tackles. Known as 'Brats' to his teammates he could also be aggressive and physically intimidating.

Half-Backs.

At the centre of the half-back line was George Robinson. Known as 'Robbo,' the miner from Hucknall, signed from Sutton Town, in June 1920, was another player with a physical presence. Robbo was loved by his teammates because of his wholehearted performances and his refusal to shirk from any physical challenge. Often underestimated because he was relatively small for a central defender, he was also an astute on-field tactician. 'Robbo' would often start games in central midfield but drop back to take a central position between the two full-backs, sometimes dropping behind goalkeeper Jack Brown to head the ball off the line. He was touched by tragedy as a young man, losing his young wife early in his marriage, probably from tuberculosis.

Robinson joined Worksop at the start of the decade as a centre-half and was soon demonstrating his defensive capability (polished and reliable in his first trial game) and his ability to score directly from set pieces. Tom

Beloved and Betrayed

Richardson, who had played with, and against, some of the top defenders in the land claimed Robinson was as good, if not better, than any centre-half he played with. 'Only his lack of inches stopped him competing with the best.'

Robbo announced himself to the Worksop supporters by curling a free-kick from distance, into the top corner of a heavily guarded goal against Mexborough, early in his inaugural season, in October 1920. After that he became chief penalty taker.

Alongside Robinson was Wilf Simmonite, another ex-Rotherham County player, also from a well-known Yorkshire footballing dynasty of footballers. Worksop's supporters were initially underwhelmed by the addition of Simmonite, fearing, correctly, that he was signed to replace one of their two great crowd favourites 'Raz' Linley (who signed for Birmingham City for £600 in December 1920 helping City to the Second Division title) and 'Sticker' Banks. However, he would soon win them over.

Simmonite always gave his all and was a talented all-round player, making timely defensive interventions that secured points, and chipping in with the occasional goal during the Midland League Championship campaign. He would prove to be an astute signing. Versatile and adaptable, occasionally playing on either wing as required.

He was destined to be an ever present on team sheets during the most successful period in the club's history. When Worksop Town desperately needed the goal that would secure their first Midland League title in a game against Mansfield Town, it was Wilf Simmonite who appeared from nowhere to slip the ball home.

Froggatt is a rugged and tidy little village in the Peak District. Froggatt Edge, a craggy gritstone escarpment, looms over the village. Both gave their name to the multiple families who share the appellation Froggatt, sons and daughters who left to explore the new opportunities afforded by the Industrial Revolution.

The two Froggatt brothers who were each a critical part of the successful Worksop squad were born in Staveley, Derbyshire. They moved with their publican father to live in the pretty village of Harthill, only a short bus ride from Worksop, when Froggatt senior became landlord of the

Blue Bell Inn. William Froggatt found work at Kiveton Colliery and played for the colliery club where he quickly established a reputation as a fearless warrior. 'Will' went straight into the Worksop first-team after he was signed on December 20th 1919 - and swiftly became a fixture, graduating to the role of vice-captain by 1923.

There was an echo of the Chapman brothers' saga decades earlier, when Worksop, for financial reasons, elected to choose between Harry and Herbert rather than taking both (correctly as Harry proved to be a slightly better player than his more famous brother, winning two League Championships and the FA Cup with the Wednesday). Worksop had planned to take just one of the Froggatt brothers, but with the strong and powerful William Froggatt established already at Worksop, Wilfred Froggatt became the top target in March 1920, after William told President Charles Longbottom that: 'Our kid can play a bit too.'

Even though some thought Wilfred's passing less effective than that of his brother, Worksop Town were soon competing with Chesterfield to sign him from junior club Harthill United. Both brothers, whilst not the most graceful of players - 'all arms and legs', as one critic described them - were strong and powerful, intimidating opponents for any team. Both soon deserved their remuneration of 25 shillings a match (about £75 at the time of writing).

On the eve of the Spurs game, Will Froggatt, vice-captain of Worksop Town faced the heartbreak of being ruled out of the most important game of his life with a 'poisoned foot.' Infections were common after minor injuries sustained in the colliery or on the pitch. Amputations sometimes followed such infections. After advice from a responsible doctor, he would be forced to watch from the bench. His replacement would be 'our kid,' his younger brother Wilf.

Forwards.

Worksop's front five were as strong as any forward line in the Midland League. Walter Robert Amos was born September 3rd 1899, in Grimsby. As a schoolboy his teacher laughed at his persistent requests to be trialled for the school team. However, once selected, Amos was a revelation and soon established himself in a successful Grimsby Boys' squad. His strength and agility were enhanced by war service with the

Lincolnshire Regiment, and he joined Grimsby Rovers in 1919 before being poached by the Worksop Town club.

Although only five feet four inches tall and nine stone eight lbs., Amos was an exceptionally gifted ball player, who was, at 24 years of age in 1923, demonstrating the self-confident trickery that would enable him to humiliate some of the best full-backs in the land during a long and successful career.

By 1933, Amos was a familiar name to football aficionados across the north of England. A Bury player, working as a columnist for the *Halifax Evening Courier*, he described how he was considered an inside-forward, either right or left before an injury and an astute piece of foresight by a Grimsby selector, saw him switched to the left wing. 'I have never regretted the change,' he concluded.

Comfortably two-footed, like Spurs winger Fanny Walden, Amos had superb balance and was capable of short bursts of speed which could be devastating when deployed against journeymen defenders in the Midland League. His skill set made him vulnerable to some brutal challenges, but his almost balletic balance enabled him to take evasive action. In his long career he would seldom be absent from a team sheet. In 1926, a close friend described Amos in the Sheffield sports paper *The Star Green 'Un*, as 'one of the pluckiest players ever to kick a ball.'

For now, as arguably Worksop's most accomplished player, he represented a serious threat to the reputation of Tom Clay, the esteemed Spurs full-back.

Thomas Rippon known as 'Pip' was, at 35 years old, a veteran campaigner and a miner who was coming to the end of his footballing career. One of two footballing brothers, Thomas and his brother Willis were from the mining village of Beighton in Derbyshire, 11 miles north-west of Worksop. Thomas and Willis were destined to become fine examples of the old football adage, 'Have boots, will travel.'

They began their career at Hackenthorpe, a village adjacent to Beighton, before moving between other clubs in the Sheffield heartlands, notably Rawmarsh Albion and Sandhill Rovers. They then moved to Kilnhurst Town, a footballing hotspot the Dearne Valley. Here a Bristol City scout spotted them.

Beloved and Betrayed

After a short sojourn in the West Country, they were offered terms in the capital. Both brothers had the distinction of being on the books of one of Spurs' many London rivals, Woolwich Arsenal in 1910. (Woolwich is in South London so the rivalry was not as intense as it is now). Thomas does not appear to have made any appearances for the Gunners first-team, but Willis played in nine games, including a 1-2 home defeat to Manchester United on September 1st 1910, and a 1-1 draw at Bury in the same year, scoring Arsenal's only goal in the latter.

From here Thomas moved north to Grimsby Town, playing for the Mariners both before and after the First World War. Rippon made 121 appearances in the Football League for Grimsby Town scoring 37 goals. In 1914 he caught, and almost died, from influenza. Initially hoping to continue his footballing career whilst working as a miner for the duration of the war, Rippon eventually joined the army.

In 1920, he joined Lincoln City, then playing in the Midland League, making his debut on August 28th 1920, in a 3–1 win at home to Mexborough Town. Rippon was the club's leading scorer in the 1920/21 season with 27 goals from League and FA Cup games. He captained Lincoln City as the Imps won the Midland League Championship. He regularly played the following season, in the newly formed Football League Third Division North, but was less prolific, though his ten goals still placed him second in Lincoln City's scoring charts. Perhaps thinking that his best years were behind him, Rippon decided to drop down to the Midland League, joining Worksop Town in the summer of 1922.

Despite his age Rippon could still lead the line with enthusiasm, energy and judgement. He remained quick over short distances and led some inspired counter-attacking charges down the centre of the field.

Thomas Lawrie was a player who attracted the attention of Football League clubs. He had already played a key role in one of Worksop's most remarkable seasons. Lawrie's goalscoring feats for the reserves brought him to the attention of the directors in October 1920. He was the man who, more than any other, represented the ebullience, team spirit and self-confidence of the 'Boys of '23.'

Although relatively small for a striker he could out jump larger opponents. Cocky, self-confident and a great raconteur - a natural comedian - Tommy provided some of the material for this book because he was destined to live longer than any other member of the team. Worksop-born Tommy lived on Kilton Road as a young man and worked underground at Manton Colliery until 1943, accepting work on the surface that year. However, despite his outward jollity, Tommy's life had been touched by tragedy. In 1921 he became the second member of the team, after George Robinson, to attend the funeral of a young wife. The cause of death is not specified in newspaper reports. It is highly likely that it was tuberculosis.

In 1923 Tommy, an enthusiastic cyclist, was supremely fit and full of confidence after playing a key role in Worksop's Midland League Championship-winning campaign and subsequent cup run. He confidently backed himself to win duels with opposing full-, and half-backs, and genuinely believed that Worksop Town would achieve the impossible at White Hart Lane.

Francis Cammack known as 'Frankie' was a Sheffield lad who started with Hallam FC before moving to Sheffield United reserves in 1920, before playing a few games for Chesterfield. Frankie was a fast and accurate crosser of the ball, and whilst not in the same league as Amos or Spink, was a generally reliable replacement on the right for the latter - Spink being more prone to injury than Amos. For him, the Spurs game would provide a once in a lifetime opportunity to participate in an important game at a major stadium.

If Only.

Worksop's chances were severely diminished by injuries sustained by their vice-captain, Will Froggatt and their two first choice strikers. Thomas William Spink was one of 'the Four Tommy's' - so called after the generic nickname given to all English soldiers in World War One, Tommy Atkins. All four were fixtures in the Worksop first eleven: Lawrie, Spink, Rippon and Cawley.

'Tommy' Spink was born on November 13th 1887, in Dipton, County Durham. At 36 he was past his peak as a player, but his signing was still perceived as a coup by the Worksop Town supporters, because he was a reliable professional who had looked after himself. The directors certainly believed that they had captured a player who would help Worksop achieve their target of Football League status.

Beloved and Betrayed

Spink had started his professional career with Grimsby Town just as the threat of war with Germany was gathering momentum. He swiftly became a firm favourite with the Mariners fans because of his pace, self-confidence and technique. A natural right-winger he posed a persistent threat on the right-hand side.

Douglas Lamming, in his book, '*A Who's Who of Grimsby Town AFC 1890-1985*' states that 'Tommy was reckoned to be one of Grimsby's best ever right-wingers because of his speed, pinpoint centring and consistency.' The 'Play Up Liverpool' website also captures a cameo of Spink's potency in this era, in a 2-2 draw with Rochdale - 'On their respective wings Spink and Smith were at times sparklingly clever; especially so was Spink, for his runs and centres were quite a feature of the second half.'

The other absent Tommy, Thomas Cawley, twice featured in Midland League end-of-season representative teams, in 1924 and 1925. Cawley's injury in 1923 was undoubtedly a serious blow to Worksop's FA Cup hopes. The combination plays between him and Amos on the left had become a definitive feature of the Worksop Town passing game.

Born in Sheffield, on November 21st 1891, Cawley came from a famous footballing family. His father played in the 1890 FA Cup Final for The Wednesday club. Tom Cawley Junior's natural home was Hillsborough, but he was not as accomplished as his father and moved to Leeds City in 1914. Unable to nail down a first-team place, he moved back to Wednesday on loan and began to make first-team appearances with the Owls.

'The Mighty, Mighty Whites' website describes the next phase of his career - 'He eventually broke through as a Leeds City regular, in the problem position on the right-wing, eight weeks later, and was a regular on the flank for the rest of the campaign, scoring six times in 26 appearances. This run included both games of the two-legged play-off for the unofficial League Championship against Stoke in May 1918. When his shot struck the bar in the first game at Elland Road, Billy Hibbert followed up to open the scoring.'

Cawley would score ten goals in 43 appearances for Leeds City. At 33 years old he had the guile and temperament of an experienced professional and was one of the Tiger's top players. As top scorer for the season, he may well have had a decisive influence on the game.

12. George Watkinson and the Herbert Chapman factor.

If you step on to a train in Worksop, heading in the direction of Sheffield, you will scarcely have time to settle in your seat before you arrive in Shireoaks, the colliery village where Michael 'Mick' Jones of Sheffield United, Leeds United and England fame honed his football skills in the 1960's. A few moments later, having passed another defunct colliery, you will arrive at Kiveton Park station. In the 1890's Kiveton was a remarkable breeding ground for footballing talent - a reluctant and grudging 'nursery' for the new Worksop Town club from the moment that they persuaded Walter Wigmore to sign as their first professional.

Harry Chapman - born February 20th 1880, took a path familiar to many. He made his debut for Kiveton in 1898 and was poached by Worksop almost immediately. In this instance the poachers soon became the poached as The Wednesday, stepped in, offering Chapman a contract in 1900. On February 23rd 1901, Chapman made his debut against Blackburn Rovers.

Harry Chapman would go on to become the top marksman in two championship seasons, winning the First Division of the Football League in 1902/03 and 1903/04. He was also man of the match as Wednesday won the FA Cup for the second time in 1907. After retiring from playing, he had a stint as Hull City manager between April 1913 and September 1914.

Tragically, Harry died of tuberculosis at the age of 36, in 1916. If the name sounds familiar, it is. Herbert Chapman, arguably the most influential football manager of all time, the manager of two legendary teams in the 1920's - Huddersfield Town and Arsenal - was Harry's brother, as was Thomas Chapman who played for Grimsby Town.

Herbert Chapman did eventually play for Worksop Town, in the critical 1900/01 season when Worksop were trying to establish themselves in the Midland League. Had he been as good a player as his younger brother he would almost certainly have played for the club before then and would probably have been part of the 1898/99 team that won the Sheffield

Beloved and Betrayed

Association league title and were runners up to the Wednesday reserves. His convoluted passage back to Sheffield to achieve his dream of playing for Sheffield United, his boyhood idols, would probably have been simpler had he had a different name.

We can only assume that Worksop overlooked his talent because they focused on comparing Harry with Herbert, and decided, correctly, that Harry had more potential as a footballer. It was not that Herbert lacked talent. He went on to play for Spurs and his record stands comparison with the best football league players that the Worksop area has produced. He made 42 appearances for Spurs scoring 16 goals.

There can be no doubt that Herbert Chapman would have been aware of the Worksop 'Donovan era' teams that achieved national recognition by beating Second Division sides, Rotherham Town and Grimsby Town, and it is hard to imagine, that with the Worksop ground only a short walk along the Chesterfield canal, he would not have attended Worksop Town games in this period.

Arthur Wharton was playing in goal for Rotherham Town when Worksop knocked them out of the FA Cup in 1893. In 1897 Wharton was the first black football manager (of Stalybridge Rovers) in the United Kingdom, and he took a chance on a young footballer from Kiveton, Herbert Chapman.

The path from Kiveton FC to Worksop FC was so well worn that it would have been surprising if Herbert had not wanted to join the coterie of Kiveton lads, like Walter Wigmore and Billy Copestake at the larger and more ambitious club within walking distance of his home village.

Later, as manager at both Huddersfield and Arsenal, Chapman won two league titles and an FA Cup. He was, as one journalist noted after his death, 'a maker of champions.' His influence on the evolution of professional football was immense, and many consider him to be the father of the modern game, adding a stadium clock, floodlights and even a white ball to the spectator experience. Many have argued that no other manager in the history of English football has ever been so innovative and influential as Chapman.

George Watkinson was already a stalwart at Worksop Town when Chapman arrived to play for the Midland League club, his new charge making an immediate impression. On October 22nd 1900, *The Sheffield Independent* reported on an FA Cup tie between Worksop Town and Doncaster Rovers which was fast paced from start to finish and was played in front of a reported but unspecified, record crowd.

Town attacked the Ryton End goal vigorously in the early stages of the game, and it was some time before Doncaster ventured outside of their own half, both teams creating, but failing to execute clear chances before half-time. In the second half, there was a critical clearance off the line by Worksop's home-grown full-back Beall, with his keeper beaten and floundering on the floor. When Worksop advanced only a remarkable save by the Doncaster keeper Egget stopped Chapman from winning the game. The game finished 0-0. The replay was equally exciting, with Chapman scoring in a 2-1 defeat. *The Sheffield Telegraph* praised his contribution: 'Hutton and Chapman, Worksop's new men both played capitally and have considerably strengthened the team.'

Chapman contributed dynamic goals and performances throughout the season, standing comparison with his brother Harry, who was performing in a lower standard of football during his spell at Worksop. He scored, home and away, in two dramatic clashes with Derby County reserves, the first a 4-4 draw and the second a 10-goal thriller. That game finished 6-4 in Derby's favour – Chapman netting a hat-trick. Chapman continued to score freely for Worksop before electing to join Northampton Town in the following season - his first step on the path to footballing immortality.

It would have been surprising if Worksop had not benefitted from the influence of such a strong personality and creative thinker as Chapman, and it is no coincidence that they produced their best finish in their history in the 1901/02 season. Finishing third in the Midland League behind the powerful reserve teams of The Wednesday and Derby County was a fine achievement and they were praised as 'the real champions,' given the near impossible task of beating First Division reserve teams that could draw on international stars in critical clashes.

WM

Many of the tactical innovations that we associate with post war football were deployed much earlier under different names.

Beloved and Betrayed

Enshrined in the folklore of football is the story of a Scottish International team of modest stature that outsmarted a taller and heavier England team with a simple trick of passing the ball to the nearest player in the same-coloured shirt. This David v Goliath feat happened at the West of Scotland Cricket ground in Partick on November 30th 1872. In the first ever international fixture, Scotland held England to a 0-0 draw.

However, it is difficult to believe that someone didn't think of this cunning plan to deprive the opposition team of the ball years earlier. There are reports of 'combination play' in a game between Sheffield Club and Hallam in 1861 and a player from Worksop, John Appleton is recorded as engaging in what was almost certainly a passing move.

In the early 1900's Worksop were one of many teams that introduced a one back system, fronted by a crowded midfield with inside forwards dropping deep. The one back was a sweeper, held back to 'sweep' up breakouts from the offside position, and push up to gain free kicks.

The moral of this story is that, in the context of football tactics, it is difficult to say for certain when a specific innovation was first employed.

In the 1920's and for decades afterwards, Worksop played the 'pyramid' system of 2,3,5. Watkinson and skipper Richardson had accrued a tremendous amount of tactical expertise from listening to Herbert Chapman and observing Ernest Needham, enough to outfox top reserve teams in winning the Midland League and develop a plan to counter the technical sophistication and attacking flair of Spurs. Richardson became a master of the craft of man marking, tackling from behind and sliding into tackles when conditions allowed.

The WM represented a simple tweak to the Pyramid system: a goalkeeper supported by two defensive full-backs behind a left-half-back, a centre-half and a right-half-back, forming a W. When the centre-half switched position, dropping back to stand between the two full backs, just before kick-off or during a game, the pattern changed to an M. This facilitated a counter-attacking style.

Watkinson and Richardson followed Herbert's career closely, as did most people in Worksop, and they paid special attention when the local heros' Huddersfield Town team prevailed in the 1922 Cup Final, deploying the

WM tactical ploy that Worksop would later use to their advantage at White Hart Lane.

13. London's finest.

Herbert Blake was a Bristolian, born on August 26th 1894. He was destined to play only one game for Bristol City before war intervened. After this, like Jimmy Seed, he was encouraged to travel over the border to the valleys of south Wales and play for Mid-Rhondda in the Southern League. This, after a failed trial with the Lancashire giants, Preston North End.

After being spotted by Spurs in 1921, Blake became an honorary Londoner, moving to the capital to enjoy two years of cosmopolitan glamour. However, it would be the more grandly named, Alexander Campbell Hunter who would be the goalkeeper of choice on April 23rd 1921, denying Blake immortality as a member of the second Spurs FA Cup winning team. It was a tough school for goalkeepers. Blake was also competing with Spurs legend, Bill Jaques (who, despite his exotic name, was born in Kent). It was only when Jaques was taken seriously ill that Blake made the position his own, going on to make 51 appearances for Spurs between 1921 and 1923.

Jaques had been 'between the sticks' for what *The Westminster Gazette* declared to be the 'Great Sheffield Debacle.' In March 1922 Spurs, as cup holders, were unexpectedly beaten by Preston North End in the FA Cup Semi-Final at Hillsborough. The 'grim, grey streets of Sheffield' seemed even greyer to the man from the *Gazette*.

Perhaps because of this defeat, Herbert Blake was destined for the singular honour of facing Worksop Town in the first round of the FA Cup campaign, a year later.

Blake's principal assets were his bravery and the outstanding power of his kicks. Like a later custodian at White Hart Lane, Pat Jennings, who once scored a famous goal against Manchester United, Herbert had the range to trouble the opposition goalkeeper from a long 'punt' downfield. His clearances too, in difficult circumstances, often received rapturous applause.

Full-backs.

The senior of the two Spurs full-backs, Thomas Clay was born in Leicester in 1892. Aged 31, he had already been a Spurs right-back for almost a decade after being signed from Leicester Fosse. We already know that the Spurs manager Peter McWilliam had an unerring eye for discovering talented young footballers, and he demonstrated astute strategic capability by moving swiftly for Clay, who was on the radar of several top teams.

In 1914 McWilliam had had the opportunity to catch Clay in competitive action when Second Division Leicester drew Spurs in the First Round of the FA Cup. Spurs prevailed over two games, but McWilliam had seen enough to swiftly secure Clay's signature.

Although the war stalled his progress, he became an established force remarkably quickly after resumption, leading Spurs to the Second Division title after being appointed as club captain in 1919. By March 1920 Clay was an England International. In the same season he endured the trauma of scoring a critical own goal, slicing the ball into his own net against Aston Villa.

Although Arthur Grimsdell was appointed club captain for the following season and had the honour of lifting the FA Cup at Stamford Bridge, Clay demonstrated consummate professionalism and mental strength in the victorious FA Cup campaign. A highly intelligent player with an exceptional ability to play the offside rule, he gave a master class in tackling and astute positional play against Wolves in the final. Faced with a fast-paced Wolverhampton attack on a treacherous Stamford Bridge pitch he was steadfast and calm.

By January 1923 he was an experienced veteran and a formidable foe for the jaunty little Worksop winger who faced him across the half-frozen White Hart Lane pitch.

Clay's partner in the penultimate line of defence was left-back John Pearson. He was a Scotsman, the same age as Clay, born in Arbroath in 1892. Pearson had joined Spurs in 1914, travelling down from his native town. During the war he served in the Royal Navy. While 1923 was to be his last season with the London club, he was unaware of this as he lined up with ten other Spurs' stars in the second week of January. Pearson was a tough, uncompromising club defender who earned the respect of all who played against him.

Half-Backs.

The half-back line were an equally formidable force. Right-half Bertram Smith was another player born in 1892, a vintage year for producing future Spurs players. 'Bert' was the fourth child of six to William and Emily. His father was an engine driver and the family lived at Wharf House in Charlton, south-east London with Bert's uncle and others.

Like many who survived childhood in this era, Bert's life was touched by tragedy: two of his siblings died in infancy.

As a player Bert was feisty and an early cult hero amongst Spurs supporters after a series of altercations with Arsenal (who rapidly became fierce rivals after 'stealing' Spurs' place in the First Division). In September 1922, *The National News and Evening Telegram* noted a typical fracas -

'After the Spurs goal came the most disgraceful scene I have witnessed on any ground at any time. Players pulled the referee, blows with fists were exchanged, and all the dignity that appertains in the referee, was rudely trampled on.'

It was serious enough to trigger a 'commission of enquiry' and Smith was suspended for a month for using 'filthy language.'

By 1923 he was an England International, after representing his country against England and Wales, and the proud owner of an FA Cup winners medal - a well respected and ambitious footballer at the peak of his career .

At centre-half, holding the middle ground, was Harry Lowe. Born in Northwich, Cheshire, in 1886, Lowe was playing for the 'Vics' when he was signed by Brighton and Hove Albion in 1913. A year later, after playing only two games on the south Coast, Harry moved north to White Hart Lane.

Lowe would play 72 matches for Spurs in all competitions between 1914 and 1926, receiving a benefit match in 1922. Lowe had failed to make the 1921 Cup Final team but forced his way back into contention in the subsequent year. At 26 years old in 1923, he was playing the best football of his career and was desperate to make amends for his disappointment in 1921 and see Tottenham reach the first Wembley final.

The final member of the middle line was a superstar of his day. Left-half Arthur Grimsdell, born in Watford, March 23rd 1894, was at the zenith of a fine career. A star for Southern League Watford FC in 1912, his exceptional ability had been noted years before as an outstanding performer at schoolboy level. Remarkably he was called up to the first-team over a decade before the Worksop game, making his Spurs debut in December 1912, before Peter McWilliam took over as manager.

Aged only 19, Grimsdell quickly caught the eye of the England selectors and played a trial for his country before war broke out. Grimsdell was one of the first footballers to volunteer to serve his country, eventually moving to the First Life Guards, and the Guard's Machine Gun regiment. A natural leader of men he was swiftly made Lance Corporal.

Grimsdell was able to play army football and returned from the war in fine shape. By May 1919 he was an England International with two caps and, in December, he was appointed to the captaincy of Spurs. In this capacity he would become the second Spurs captain to lift the FA Cup. An attacking midfielder with a fierce shot, and an astute and intimidating defender, Arthur was an asset at both ends of the pitch. He was an inspirational figure with an international reputation, on and off the pitch. It would have been surprising if the Worksop Town players had not been a little daunted by the prospect of facing him.

Forwards. The Famous Five.

To anyone who followed top-class football live, on the radio or in the sporting press, the Spurs front five presented a dazzling, intoxicating and intimidating array of talent. It was clear why the popular press and even *The Times* referred to them as the 'Mighty' Spurs.

James Henry Dimmock was a real local hero, a son of Edmonton, born December 5th 1900. He was, at 22 years of age, still a fresh-faced, young-looking left-winger who had signed for Spurs at 18, having been associated with the club since he was a schoolboy. Towards the end of the war, he was loaned to Clapton Orient, to finely tune his skills, before signing a professional contract in 1919. Both Clapton Orient and, more significantly, Arsenal, had wanted to sign him but his heart was already at White Hart Lane and his boots would soon follow.

It was Dimmock's winning goal in the 1921 Cup Final, on a slippery and dangerous Stamford Bridge surface, which enshrined him in Tottenham's rich history, the Spurs youngster striking for immortality from the edge of the area against Wolves. He was subsequently chosen to represent his country against Scotland - the first of three caps. A supremely fit young man, he was ever present in league and cup fixtures other than a game he missed playing for England.

Dimmock's poise and balance made him a nightmare for any defender. Keeping his eyes keenly on the ball he could leave the finest British right-backs floundering as he delivered a perfect cross for the predatory Spurs strikers to take full advantage of.

At inside-left, Charles Harold James Handley aka Charlie or 'Titch', born Edmonton, March 12th 1899, was another Edmonton youth player who excelled after he joined his local club, Spurs in 1922. Developing his skills playing football in his back garden, Handley was a prodigious goal-scorer as a youngster and continued to score as well as deliver goals on a plate for his fellow strikers, with penetrating passes from the left. Handley was a player who could be trusted to play adequately in almost every position on the pitch.

Alexander Findlay Lindsay, born in Dundee, November 8th 1896, was one of many Scottish strikers who have graced Spurs over the years. A favourite of the Spurs fans and a faithful servant to the club, the Dundonian was a natural footballer, versatile enough to shine in any position.

Starting with Dundee Violet, Lindsay moved to Raith Rovers before being signed by Spurs in 1919. He remained with Spurs for a decade. At just five foot and seven and a half inches, he was small for a centre-forward, but he led a forward line that shared goals out equably with aplomb, orchestrating moves as well as finishing clinically himself.

Lindsay was another victim of Tottenham's embarrassment of riches in 1921. He missed the Cup Final so was desperate to complete the journey to Wembley in 1923.

Beloved and Betrayed

At inside-right the incomparable Jimmy Seed, was, arguably, the person who contributed most to making the twenties one of Tottenham's most successful decades.

Completing the dazzling array of talent facing Worksop's full and half-backs, was another superstar of his day. The diminutive Frederick Ingram Walden was, at only five feet two inches, one of the smallest top flight footballers in history but his consummate skillset was extensive enough to embarrass, and sometimes, humiliate, the best footballers in the land.

Walden was anointed 'Fanny' by his school friends at Wellingborough school - named after the woman who ran the school shop. From the start the little boy demonstrated that he had the heart of a Lion. In 1905 he received a special award from the Prince of Wales, later King George V, for saving a boy from drowning.

Fanny Walden was the oldest campaigner in the team, born in the east Midlands, at Wellingborough in 1888. The man who is seldom far from our story, Herbert Chapman, can be credited with recognising that the exceptional talent of Walden could grace the finest stadiums despite the vulnerability of his apparent frailty and stature. Walden had already had a substantial junior and non-league career when he came under the influence of Chapman, who had recently moved to Northampton from Worksop Town.

Soon poached by a team with even more potential, Chapman was desperate for Walden to move to Leeds City with him in 1912, but Northampton resisted. It was the financial power of Tottenham and the persuasive charm of their manager, the astute Peter McWilliam, that enabled Spurs to frustrate Chapman and secure his signature in 1913. Walden would go on to represent his country - the smallest player ever to play for England at football.

Although he was coming to the end of his career in 1923 the prospect of facing a player with such exceptional grace, poise and balance allied to fearsome pace, would have disturbed the sleep of almost any defender in the world.

The Boss.

Peter McWilliam was already a football legend before he was appointed to take over a Tottenham Hotspur team that had floundered since his fellow Scot, the great John Cameron who led Southern League Spurs to their first FA Cup Final success, had left the club in 1907.

McWilliam had captained his country and been a key part of a great Newcastle United side that reached four FA Cup Finals (winning one) whilst securing three league titles in only five years between 1905 and 1910. He was a leader and proven winner.

McWilliam's greatest attribute was his exceptional ability to assess a footballer's overall potential, which facilitated his capacity to sign players from lower league clubs at 'bargain' prices and see them evolve into stars of the national game.

On the pitch he encouraged his players to become active participants in analysing games tactically. His senior players were trusted to make decisions on the field, subsequently becoming adept at changing systems and player positions and often changing the course of a game in favour of Spurs. It worked – McWilliam's Spurs won the cherished prize of the FA Cup in 1921 and came within six points of the First Division title in 1922. The champions of the Midland League would be facing perhaps the best, and certainly the most glamorous club in the land, with one of their greatest managers plotting their inevitable downfall.

The Donovans (RA)

The Shamrocks 1908/09 (TC)

W. LILLY,

Match box sold for the William (Bill) Lilley testimonial.

Note the incorrect spelling of his name (SD)

1920s Worksop Town tie (LR)

Tom Richardson circa 1923 (TC)

Jack Brown: a painting by Alan Rolfe

Jimmy Seed: a painting by Alan Rolfe

Wilf Froggatt's Challenge Cup medal (MF)

September 2019:

John Stocks, Mavis Froggatt and Lance Hardy.

Mavis is the daughter of Wilf.

(MH)

Worksop Town FC, May 1922 (WG)

G Watkinson, G Limb, G Raines, WE Davies (Vice-Chair), WF Longbottom, WG Davies, JW Caseldine, F Hensley, R Martin, *not known*

AJ Tomlinson (chair), T Farmer, G Newton, G Huxford, W Froggatt, Albert (Bert) Foreman, T Moore, B Pardon, J Machin, GH Storer, FG Foster

Will Mercer, Jack Tremelling, George Webster, Horace Bratley, Wilf Froggatt, George Robinson, Tom Richardson, Jack Brown, Will Gee, Billy Marshall

T Slater, Bill Edson, Fred Banks, Tom Lawrie, Arthur Charlesworth, Wilf Simmonite, Wally Amos, William (Bill) Lilley, Jack Barton

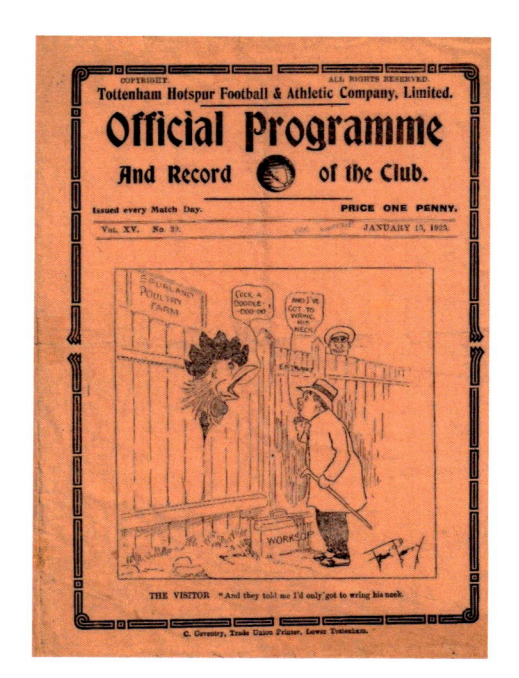

Tottenham Hotspur v Worksop Town

FA Cup First Round Replay

(BG)

A sketch by Paul Wyer from the first game at White Hart Lane (PW)

14. Destiny Calls.

Hewers and Heroes.

In the quarter of a century since 1898, only two teams had inflicted home defeats in the FA Cup on the mighty Spurs - Aston Villa, on two occasions and Blackburn Rovers. If the Tottenham players felt any pressure prior to kick off it was because they were not only expected to complete the termination of Worksop's cup campaign, but to provide a feast of goals, and perhaps a record score to entertain the crowd. They were aware that Chelsea had put nine goals in the back of the Worksop net in 1908 and expected to do at least as well. Hence the look of steely-eyed determination on the face of Arthur Grimsdell, the Spurs Captain.

Telegram offering good luck and best wishes to Worksop Town (CF)

The Worksop players, granted a fantastic reception from a warm-hearted Tottenham crowd, were lost in the moment. They stood gazing in awe, as sudden, simultaneous flashes of light from 20 thousand lucifer matches illuminated the towering stands of White Hart Lane, the plumes of smoke drifting up the terraces to join the miasma of toxic smog already drifting south to the heart of London Town. It was a formidable and mesmerising sight.

Peter McWilliam was too wily an operator to take any challenge lightly - when a reporter suggested that Worksop had little chance of an upset, McWilliam replied in the colloquial words of his father: 'Facts are chiels that winna ding,' (Things that cannot be disputed). Adding, 'And the facts are that Worksop are the best side in the Midland League. I am told that Worksop are basing their hopes on a draw at White Hart Lane and then a replay at Worksop.'

The prevailing mood amongst the crowd was one of light-hearted jocularity - they would be happy to cheer any flashes of inspiration from the Worksop players amidst the deluge of inevitable goals for Spurs. Bill Lilley, 'Old Bill', still in his mid-twenties, but, after his war trauma, looking at least ten years older, was used to good natured joshing from his teammates so knew there was no malice in the laughter and calls of 'take it easy Grandad' from the Spurs supporters, but the sheer scale of the ridicule from thousands of bobbing heads was disconcerting.

At 2.30 pm, with a thin mist still swirling around the ground, and the pitch scarcely taking a stud, the game commenced with an exchange between the two 'Tommys' who had made it on to the White Hart Lane turf.

Worksop started proceedings, defending the Edmonton goal. Rippon kicked off and passed to Lawrie, who executed a perfect pass to a tiny figure on the wing. The crowd applauded the basic move generously. Wally Amos controlled the ball with consummate ease and set off down the wing. Tom Clay sized up the tiny figure scooting cheerfully towards him with the ball at his feet, coolly. He did not know him from Adam and, even if he had done due diligence on his opponent, he could not have known that, on January 1st 1925, Wally Amos would be playing for a Bury team seven places above Spurs in the second division and ripping the Spurs defence apart, missing a penalty and scoring a fine hat-trick, in a 5-2 home victory.

As Amos outflanked him with arrogant ease the crowd laughed at Clay's bewildered discomfort and Amos's jaunty audacity. Clay frowned and resolved to wipe the smug smile off his face.

Beloved and Betrayed

White Hart Lane, Tottenham, London, 1923

Tottenham Hotspur

1 Herbert Blake

2 Thomas Clay 3 John Pearson

4 Herbert Smith   5 Harry Lowe   6 Arthur Grimsdell

8 Jimmy Seed   10 Charles Handley

7 Fanny Walden   9 Alex Lindsay   11 Jimmy Dimmock

Manager: Peter McWilliam

Worksop Town

1 Jack Brown

2 Horace Bratley   5 George Robinson   3 Thomas Richardson

4 Wilfred Simmonite   6 Wilfred Froggatt

8 Thomas Lawrie   10 William Lilley

7 Francis Cammack   9 Thomas Rippon   11 Walter Amos

Trainer: George Watkinson

Referee: RE Small   Attendance: 21,928

Receipts: £1,445 14s 4d

But as Rippon hurtled down the centre it was the Worksop supporters' turn to take a reality check - Amos's cross floated hopelessly behind the goal. The crowd laughed.

The Tottenham players found their passing rhythm quickly, fizzing the ball around the midfield with impunity. The Worksop half-backs, well drilled by Watkinson, focused on keeping their shape and watching the passage of the ball carefully.

Next, Horace Bratley swept forward, clattering unceremoniously into Seed. It looked clumsy but the Worksop players knew better - 'Brats' was passing over his calling card, letting the Tottenham star know he was here.

The subsequent free-kick set a template for the game. Robinson dropped deep but the free-kick was hit wide - Bratley slipped slightly on the frozen surface, but the compact figure of Wilf Simmonite was watching his back and he controlled the ball and cleared downfield. The remorseless covering and double covering of the Worksop Town defensive unit, three half-backs and two full-backs, would frustrate the momentum of the Spurs attacks in the early stages. The *Daily Mirror* reporter noted the pattern.

'Spurs wanted to show no mercy but the 'Collier Boys' were quicker on the ball and one player covered another - several others. They were magnificent in this respect.'

Then, as Frankie Cammack advanced on the right, the Spurs half-backs looked surprised at the pace of the Worksop reserve but, with Rippon again hurtling into the goal area, Cammack mis-timed his cross.

Spurs settled and began to pass and move again, but the Worksop half-backs, and full-backs were undaunted. They were used to frustrating the talented reserve sides of The Wednesday, Sheffield United and Nottingham Forest, and, to a man, they kept their shape, slipping effortlessly behind each other and forcing the Tottenham players to shoot from distance.

Speculative shots from Lindsay and Handley were well wide. After 20 minutes of robust combative play Jack Brown had not had a shot to save. Jimmy Seed and Arthur Grimsdell, were seen deep in conversation, surveying the pitch in frustration, trying to ascertain what the problem was.

They were unlikely to work out the conundrum that had its roots in the relationship between George Watkinson and a man destined to become Spurs' nemesis by the end of the decade, the ex-Worksop Town and Tottenham Hotspur star, Herbert Chapman. Although they had not been colleagues for many years, Watkinson followed Chapman's career closely. In discussion with the acclaimed biographer of Chapman, Patrick Barclay, Lance Hardy discovered that Chapman had used his centre-back Tom Wilson in a 'spoiling role' between the two full-backs in the 1922 Cup Final when he was manager of Huddersfield Town. George Watkinson had taken note.

WORKSOP back heads away a very dangerous shot. The visitors played a sound and vigorous game. The light was bad.

BROWN, Worksop's goalkeeper, just saves from a hot shot. Spurs attacked strongly towards the interval, but without success.

Sunday Pictorial, Tottenham Hotspur v Worksop Town (SP)

Worksop play the WM.

It was Grimsdell who first noticed the tactical innovation, Worksop were using a strategic ploy scarcely seen in England until 1925, when it was used so impressively by Herbert Chapman's all conquering Arsenal team and was subsequently recognised as one of the most significant structural transformations in football history. The Worksop plan was to contain first, by defending in depth and using the acceleration and erratic ball skills of Frankie Cammack on one wing, and the pace and guile of Wally Amos on the other. They would launch rapid counter attacks targeting 'Pip' Rippon, racing down the middle.

Beloved and Betrayed

The two inside-forwards Lawrie and Lilley, both more comfortable with a predatory striking role - would drop back creating the W shape formed by the positioning of the front five players. George Robinson would take the 'withdrawn centre-half' role, creating, effectively, a new tactical system, 3-2-5, the M formed from the movement of the back 5. This effectively became 3-4-3 with the two inside-forwards expected to drop back and support the half-backs. It worked. *The Daily Mail* reporter noted how Amos and Cammack 'frequently troubled Clay and Pearson.' All the reports noted how obdurate the Worksop defensive system was, and how Spurs found difficulty in creating chances.

Grimsdell decided that with centre-half Robinson holding the Worksop fort so effectively, Spurs needed to counter with an extra-man, so he pushed himself further forwards, indicating to Dimmock that he should cover him if necessary. Grimsdell surged through the middle, but the ball ran away from him on the smooth surface. Seed manoeuvring cleverly in midfield managed to find space, but he too was forced to shoot from distance. Brown dashed out and cleared smartly. After 20 minutes of play it was the first time he had touched the ball.

A superb tackle by Robinson stopped Lindsay in his tracks, while another Wally Amos run left Smith for dead as Worksop counter attacked aggressively appreciating that Grimsdell's advanced role provided opportunities. Lindsay burst through the middle, but Brown came dashing out of goal bravely to clear, although forcing him to leave his goal exposed. Handley shot powerfully towards the open goal and the Worksop supporters held their breath, only for the withdrawn centre-back Robinson to appear and head the ball over the bar.

Tom Richardson marshalled his defence efficiently for the corner. It was swiftly repelled, and with Grimsdell desperately racing back, Wally Amos and Bill Lilley countered in tandem, outpacing the Spurs defence again and getting them into what one journalist described as a 'hopeless tangle.' It was only a superbly timed, 'last ditch' tackle by Grimsdell that saved the day for Spurs.

Clay required a fortuitous bounce of the ball to halt an aggressive Rippon charge, and Tommy Lawrie, relishing a break from defensive duties, looked to be through, before being called back for offside.

Spurs finally conjured a goal-scoring opportunity just as the half was drawing to a close. Fanny Walden and Seed were a double act that had destroyed many of the most competent defences in the land and after a burst of typical Walden dribbling, balance and close control, Bratley was left swinging his left boot at fresh air. The cross was inch perfect, and Seed made good contact, only for the ball to fly just over the bar.

Despite this, it was to be the Tigers that finished the half on the front foot. Frankie Cammack, the player from the 'stiffs' who spent most of his time playing against village teams in the Portland League and who'd been amazed to find himself on the same pitch as London's finest, had settled down on the right and was ready to play his part. On 40 minutes he raced towards the captain of England, Arthur Grimsdell, with the ball at his feet, swerved past him and, looking up, saw Rippon and Lawrie, both with an arm raised, hurtling into the penalty area. He hit a near perfect cross and the two 'Tommys' were only inches away.

The Worksop players trooped off, laughing and joking in a stadium that was a sea of smiles. Worksop had put up a good show. The crowd reflected on how, when they tired, in the second half, and Spurs ripped them apart, they could be sure of a warm reception .

There were stern words in the Spurs dressing room. Grimsdell said that the performance had been 'embarrassing.' They all needed to raise their game and teach these upstarts a lesson. The Worksop dressing room saw Tom Richardson clapping his hands and forcefully repeating his mantra. 'You can't beat em.' He was referring to his own boys, not the Tottenham Hotspur team.

Hewers and Heroes. Second Half.

The Tottenham supporters expected a reaction and a different story in the second half and Walden delivered a flying start. Effortlessly slipping past three Worksop players with a shimmy and a feint of his hips, he delivered a perfect cross which Robinson headed out for a corner. Once again Worksop's positioning and man marking was as good as any seen at White Hart Lane during the season. *The Daily Mail* would describe 'their coolness and resourcefulness under pressure.'

The ball was comfortably cleared, and a Richardson pass sent Tommy Rippon bursting through the centre. The burly miner was a fearsome sight in full flight, and he was only stopped by a brilliant tackle from Lowe, just over the half way line.

Next a series of brilliant passes from Grimsdell, Seed and Lindsay swept Spurs down the field. Seed's pass put Lindsay through, and he looked certain to score until Bratley appeared from nowhere and delivered a perfectly timed and decisive tackle.

Spurs were having their best spell of the game. Worksop were forced to concede a corner and once again Brown dashed out to punch clear leaving his goal exposed, this time it was Richardson who covered, clearing off the line.

Worksop were tackling fiercely and conceding free-kicks. Grimsdell had two with the goal in his sights, but both went over the bar. Spurs had clearly stepped up a gear and the lilywhite shirts were driving forwards with real intent. Walden was starting to be a torment on the wing, teasing and provoking Bratley into mistakes like a matador toying with a mad bull. Three times he left him for dead, sending perfect crosses spinning into the area. Twice Robinson and Richardson won aerial duels and Seed headed just wide from a third.

Worksop were briefly under siege, tackling for their lives, and, if beaten, doubling back to cover the next man. The journeyman Simmonite saved a certain goal, putting his body on the line to charge down a shot from Lindsay who then put his second chance over the bar.

The Daily Mail reported the 'amazing dash and energy' of the half-backs 'Froggatt, Simmonite and Robinson.' Even at this late stage, Tottenham were not having it all their own way. Wally Amos and Bill Lilley broke away, sweeping passes to each other superbly but support came too late. Faced with another surge from 'Pip' Rippon, Handley and Lindsay had a 'Keystone Cop's collision,' bowling each other over to laughter from the crowd.

Once again Rippon cut through the centre of the Spurs' defence and was only stopped when he was bowled over by a desperate challenge from Clay. Cammack, who was having the game of his life, outpaced Herbert Smith. From the subsequent cross, Rippon only missed by inches. Spurs keeper Blake then had to make a desperate charge out of his goal to thwart another Tigers attack.

Beloved and Betrayed

The crowd cheered Worksop's first corner generously. Amos curled the ball in and Dimmock, unused to defensive duties, panicked, slicing the ball back towards his own goal when attempting to clear. A header from the bald head of 'old Bill' Lilley was just wide of the Spurs goal.

With the clock ticking down, and the crowd scarcely able to believe their eyes, Frankie Cammack, neatly dispossessed left-back John Pearson and hit the most perfect through ball of his life, splitting the Spurs defence in half. It landed at the feet of Bill Lilley who, perhaps surprised by Cammack's precision, was faced with a tap-in for immortality. He was still a predatory finisher and was known as 'One Shot' because he liked to hit the ball first time.

But on this occasion Lilley hesitated, controlled the ball, and as he turned to shoot was charged off it by a desperate challenge from Smith. Spurs had survived.

Then in the dying moments of the game, Lowe found himself in space with plenty of time to aim and shoot at Jack Brown's goal. He struck the ball perfectly, low and hard into the penalty area. It looked to be game over, until Brown flung himself to the corner and saved the day with a spectacular catch .

The Worksop Town players in their amber and black striped shirts and white shorts walked slowly off the pitch savouring the generous wholehearted approbation of the Spurs' supporters and the cheers of their own fans. The Tottenham players, in contrast, looked shaken but relieved to have lived to fight another day.

When they got to the dressing room the Worksop celebrations were wild and uproarious - the directors came racing down the steep main-stand steps throwing their hats in their air and 'whooping' as they rushed down to greet the boys in the dressing room. Tom Haydock did a step dance, which *The Worksop Guardian* described as 'toned up to concert pitch.' The directors linked arms and danced a jig, the mining lads sang salacious ballads.

The only note of regret came with a shake of the head from a Worksop director who said - 'If only we'd had Spink !'

15. Glory Boys. The Magnificent Miners.

'It was magnificent.' The superlative appears repeatedly in reports from a century ago. 'A magnificent performance.'

'Spurs wanted to show no mercy but the 'Collier Boys' were quicker on the ball and one player covered another, several others, they were magnificent in this respect.'

'They defended as 'a solid phalanx.' If one player was beaten then another slotted in to take his place, and if he was beaten there was always another.'

The Saturday Specials and the Sunday papers mined the obvious seams of affectionate but patronising collier clichés. The boys were 'a gallant set of triers' and 'whole-hearted workers' whilst missing the point that the players had obviously transferred the solidarity of the work-place to the football field. Working in incredibly difficult and dangerous conditions, day and night, the miners had to focus and watch each other's backs constantly.

They did it instinctively - their lives depended on teamwork and trust. They were, in the words of the man from *The Times*. 'The men who came from the bowels of the earth, nine men who had hewn coal at local pits two days before, and a clerk and a bricklayer.'

'Straight out of the coal mines they came.' announced *The Daily Sketch*.

'Nine of the men from Worksop had been working underground' announced *The Times*, conjuring up an image of the Worksop lads crawling out of the depths just before kick-off.

The Spurs players were drawn into the inevitable stereotyping too, even though many were 'working-class-lads-made-good' themselves. *The Times* described the Spurs players as 'massaged and manicured.' It is not hard to imagine Jimmy Seed's response to that patronising comment.

Worksop Town FC were the story of the day, having held the footballing giants, 'Spurs' to a 0-0 draw on their own turf. The newspapers agreed, as one, that 'seldom has a greater sensation been caused in the football world.' For a fleeting period, Worksop were 'the Darlings of the Nation.' The fact that they were largely a team of miners added spice to the story. Reporters were despatched from the Metropolis to find out more about the lives of these men who had who crawled out of the pit to put on a show of dash, pluck, speed and stamina.

There was also a general acceptance that it was not a fluke. The conditions, a hard surface, and a light ball suited Worksop's players but only because they were more willing to put their bodies on the line. They wanted it more. *The Daily Telegraph* described the Tiger's performance as 'one of the most remarkable exhibitions of grit and perseverance seen on a London football field.' Full-backs Horace Bratley and skipper Tom Richardson gave the Spurs' wingers a tough afternoon, they denied them time on the ball to express their skills, and 'Mr George Robinson,' 'the inimitable Robbo' as one journalist described him, controlled the centre midfield like a general.

The Daily Mail reporter reflected on how Bratley and Richardson 'never had the slightest hesitation' in making tackles and how the defence was ' too quick for the Spurs' forwards' and how they 'never looked like breaking down.'

The man from *The Times*, Russell Stannard was full of praise for the men who came up from the 'pits' and 'gave Spurs 45 minutes of desperate football.'

The 'brawny miner' with the 'nickname Robbo' gained Stannard's warmest accolades as he reflected that, according to the Worksop directors, 'Robbo' had: 'Lately been spending his working hours toiling down the pit in a three-foot hole.'

Bratley played the 'one back in quite the best manner of Clay.' And Wilf Simmonite also caught his eye, being 'determined not to be beaten by the Seed/Walden combination' and 'did marvellously against those adroit tacticians Handley and Dimmock.'

The Sheffield Telegraph concluded that 'if Worksop had had the least bit of luck, they would have created a sensation.' *The Daily Sketch* stated 'that Spurs did not deserve to win.'

The Daily Telegraph pointed out that, 'On a slippery surface, Spurs were often in trouble, seldom Worksop.' Most of the London papers agreed that Town could, and perhaps should, have won. *The Guardian* noted that the Tottenham supporters, to their credit, 'cheered Worksop to the echo' and praised Worksop's own 'lusty lunged' supporters.

Beloved and Betrayed

It was *The Daily Sketch* that left an indelible impression of the final moments, noting how the Spurs' fans rose as one to 'applaud a team of footballers who represented all that is best in English sport.'

Later, Post Office workers in London attached messages of congratulation on parcels bound for Worksop.

Hindsight is a Wonderful Thing.

Years later, in 1976, an old man with a sparkle in his eye, sipped his pint in the Worksop Miner's Welfare club as his thoughts drifted back to that momentous day in his youth. The sprightly old chap who was still able to use his bicycle was Tommy Lawrie - the last surviving Tiger from the team of 1923. He spoke passionately about the moment that defined the tie, to *The Worksop Guardian* reporter, Mel Bradley.

'I'm certain' said Lawrie, 'if Bill Lilley had hit Frankie Cammack's cross first time, he'd have scored. But he tried controlling the ball, a yard out of goal!'

Tommy worked at Manton Colliery. He lived at 139 Kilton Road, and he earned six shillings a day, plus three pounds, ten shillings, from his football pay. He was a happy go-lucky chap with few regrets. He spurned the chance to go full time with Mansfield because it would have meant a drop in earnings. Tommy remembered the game as clearly as if it had been yesterday.

'It was a frozen pitch, we risked things the Spurs didn't. We had nothing to lose and everything to gain.'

In the Blue Bell pub at Harthill the 'Boys of '23' occasionally gathered in the snug, to reminisce about 'the Roaring Twenties,' the ever-diminishing band of brothers still relishing the sweetness of being fondly remembered local heroes.

Vice-captain, Will Froggatt, condemned by injury to watching from the bench, reflecting on one of the defining moments of the first game many years later said, 'Bill Lilley had the chance to walk up to the goal keeper Blake and ask him where he wanted it putting.' Adding that, 'He was too surprised and let the chance go by.'

Back home in Worksop after the game, there was euphoria, and impromptu dancing as the news came through by telegram. At Central

Avenue, where a schoolboy game was taking place, regular wires from White Hart Lane had kept everyone informed. A game between Carlton United and Worksop Territorials paused as the half-time score came through.

At Hillsborough stadium, Sheffield, a large crowd stayed on after the Wednesday fixture, waiting in tense expectation, and cheered wildly when the result was announced. The famously strong ales of the enormous Worksop and Retford Brewery, which loomed over the town imperiously, were poured long past official closing time. Troubles were forgotten.

The national press carried the story on front as well as back pages, *The Daily Mirror* publishing photographs of Jack Brown on its back page. Brown, a full-time miner, had no intimation that he was destined to become the first of three goalkeepers who represented Worksop Town to play for England (the others being 1960s Sheffield United keeper, Alan Hodgkinson and Aaron Ramsdale).

'One of the most remarkable exhibitions of grit and perseverance seen on a London football field for many a long day was given by the miners of Worksop Town at White Hart Lane, where Tottenham Hotspur had to be content with a draw,' the Daily Telegraph reported.

Apart from a few who refused to believe their own eyes and chose to prioritise Worksop's luck and Spurs' profligate shooting, the majority acknowledged that Worksop's defensive performance was not a fluke but a well-drilled and coherent strategy. *The Westminster Gazette* described Worksop as 'safe and sure in defence.' The Sunday Illustrated reported Bratley and Richardson as 'head and shoulders above the rest, neither put a foot wrong.' The Daily Telegraph went as far as to say that, 'A finer line of defence has not been seen in London this year.'

And this was no surprise to the players, supporters, and directors of Worksop Town. A club that had stayed unbeaten for over a season at any professional level, must have established an assured composure, and a variety of tactics to mitigate against individual error.

16. Triumph and Disaster.

Worksop supporters firmly believed that their side could knock out Spurs at home, especially with the advantage of local knowledge of their mercurial Central Avenue pitch. Central Avenue, surrounded by water from the River Ryton and the Chesterfield canal, could be fast and slippery on the wings and claggy in the middle. Two of their previous Football League victims dismissed by the Tigers, mentioned the intense atmosphere generated by the club's supporters. There was talk of tickets, the price of them and a once-in-a-life-time experience at the club's 8,000 capacity ground in the heart of the town.

The supporters had demonstrated during previous home ties that they could fill the ground, even when prices were significantly raised and with the unique attraction of an historic visit from one of the most famous and glamorous clubs in the land to relish, there was talk, as there had been at Southend, of handing over blank cheques to the secretary.

The players believed in miracles too. When asked about their chances in the replay, Tom Richardson, playing up to his press audience, but sounding relaxed and confident said, 'We'll beat the beggars.'

When asked whether he had been intimidated facing Fanny Walden, he said, 'I wanted to pick him up and put him in my pocket.'

The Tottenham Hotspur Office, White Hart Lane, London, 4.30pm.

As soon as the game was over a three-man sub-committee of Worksop Town directors, headed by the Chairman Albert John Tomlinson gathered in the club office of the White Hart Lane stadium, to make, arguably, the most important decision of their lives. Club minutes show that the sub-committee, responsible for all the arrangements for the Spurs game had been AJ Tomlinson's idea, and that the other directors had approved it.

It is highly unlikely that the Spurs' directors had considered that a meeting would be necessary, but the speed with which it was convened suggests that there had been some discussion beforehand about what would happen if a replay was required.

Chairman AJ Tomlinson, FG Hensley representing the Manton Colliery club with which Worksop Town were affiliated, and secretary Harry

Beloved and Betrayed

Storer were given the authority to make decisions on behalf of the full board. It was a simple decision about where to play the replay, but at the same time it was a call that went straight to the 'soul' of football.

Worksop Town directors. Chairman Tomlinson is seated.
The poster is advertising a 1922 game against Southend (TC).

Tomlinson had played for the club in the early years and had been a committee member since 1894. Harry Storer had joined the committee in 1907, before becoming treasurer in 1910/11 and secretary from 1912. Both were steeped in the history and heritage of the club and felt emboldened to make the big calls on game switches. They were both in situ when, having been drawn at home to Chelsea in 1908, the game was switched to Stamford Bridge.

A decade later, in 1933, Harry Storer wrote a letter to *The Sheffield Telegraph* in which he said there had been a 'tape machine' in the office and the three Worksop directors sat with their Spurs counterparts waiting for results to come through. As they did so, eyebrows were raised on both sides of the table. An unprecedented tally of 12 drawn games in the First Round remains, to this day, a bizarre statistical anomaly.

At some point Albert Tomlinson stuck out his hand indicating that he was willing to strike a deal and stated that they would not return home but would stay in London for the weekend and play the replay on Monday. It was a decision that would haunt him for the rest of his life.

Tomlinson claimed draws necessitating other replays 'helped in the director's decision to stay in London for the replay.' Perhaps, but there was no replay in Nottingham or Sheffield planned for Thursday 18th, (a half day holiday in Worksop) and the Forest ground was free all week. Responding to a charge in *The Worksop Guardian* that they responded, 'hastily and unwisely,' he stated that 'they considered pros and cons most carefully.' The Tottenham directors offered a 'take it or leave it' deal and insisted the Worksop trio made a swift decision.

At its best the FA Cup is a story of fate and destiny, the winners determined by degrees of luck and good fortune as well as skill, strength and panache. A run of favourable home draws and key rivals forced to face each other in early rounds can facilitate the unheralded progress of teams to the steps of Wembley Stadium.

The process of picking balls from a hat, prayers offered for a home draw or an away game in one of the cathedrals of British football history, provides an emotive back drop to every giant-slaying tale. To interfere with this sacred process has always seemed frustrating and cynical to any true lover of football, and, when entwined with bribery and corruption, nefarious.

The capability for self-reflection of these men is difficult to gauge. Tomlinson was a self-made man who appears to have been defined by pragmatism. Did he pause to consider whether he would find himself on the right side of history? Did he just see pound notes floating before his eyes? Or reflect on whether football was just another game played with a ball, played to the rules of Association Football as defined in the dictionary, or something richer, deeper, more emotionally charged. He was undoubtedly a football man, having been involved with the club for most of his life, but, to the real football supporter, the FA Cup was already glistening with 'the stuff that dreams are made of.' Did the financial inducement include a 'backhander' (today, referred to as a bung) to the directors, and possibly the players, that stretched his resistance to temptation to breaking point?

For all the romance, football has always been a business. A business tainted with lies, deceit and corruption from the moment, in the amateur era, when the first pound note had been surreptitiously stuffed into the coat pocket of a gentleman - inducing them to switch sides for material gain. Worksop FC had successfully persuaded dangerous local rivals such as Wath and Staveley to switch FA Cup ties in the 19th century. Jimmy Seed, unsurprisingly, had already developed a cynical view of the game. In his autobiography he stated that: 'The cheque book ruled football.'

Seed went on to proclaim that corruption, and intended corruption, was rife in the period leading up to the First World War and continued to be widespread in the post-war era. The business of professional football had been erratically regulated from the start, and even today it provides a haven for rapacious charlatans and speculative investors devoid of a moral compass.

The Dressing Room. White Hart Lane. 5.30pm.

The Worksop Town players had been locked in the dressing room for an hour. Tension was rising. The initial euphoria had temporarily dissipated as they began to speculate about what was taking place in the tiny office beneath the main stand. As experienced campaigners they were aware of the nature of the discussion that they were unable to influence. But they knew what they desperately wanted - to bring the Spurs home to Worksop.

Beloved and Betrayed

Without making too big a leap of the imagination we can visualise them praying for news of a journey back to Worksop on the mail train from Kings Cross - excitement increasing as they arrived at Retford where a small crowd had driven over from Worksop to be the first to greet them, with news of hundreds more waiting at Worksop station to similarly receive their heroes on their return home. There would be the easily discerned pride of their families. Perhaps a dispensation from the mine owners to allow them to prepare during the week and then a replay at Worksop on the Thursday in front of a sold-out, passionate, and raucous home-crowd - an opportunity to create the greatest FA Cup shock of all time.

It was probably captain Tom Richardson who was given the onerous task of breaking the news that the directors had agreed to replay the tie, on Monday, January 15th at White Hart Lane. The players appear to have been forbidden from voicing their opinion, but we know that the mood amongst the players changed swiftly from jubilation to a mixture of confusion, sorrow, disappointment and anger.

There were rumours of fights amongst the players after the decision was announced. Eventually anger turned to resignation. They knew their place in the decision-making hierarchy of the Worksop club. It reflected their place in the wider social class system. They also knew, from experience, that if they argued too vociferously, or even offered an opinion, they could find themselves without a football team to play for, some might even lose their job at Manton Colliery. They would just have to like it or lump it.

A local miner ,who drank with some of the players, remembered one saying, on several occasions, 'It was like being asked to climb Mount Everest twice in three days. We were broken.'

In voting to let head preside over heart were these men sticking a dagger into the latter, killing a thing of beauty, a dream that is unquantifiable in financial terms - a precious story that could have given pleasure to generations and can never be retrieved? Or were they simply focused on getting the maximum financial renumeration for their club?

17. Saturday Night and Sunday Morning.

Piccadilly. Saturday, January 13th 10.30pm.

Inevitably there was a party. Enough supporters stayed for a second night for *The Worksop Guardian* to report on scenes in the fashionable heart of London.

Wilf Simmonite recalled how, alongside other players, he was chaired shoulder-high in admiration around Leicester Square and Piccadilly Circus that evening, the two iconic venues described as 'a sea of amber and black' in *The Worksop Guardian*. The reporter said he had to rub his eyes 'to make sure it was Piccadilly and not Bridge Street' (Worksop's principal thoroughfare).

Tommy Lawrie recalled the generosity of 'the Cockneys' who plied them with free-drinks on a night that would live long in memory and joked about the 'crawl' back to the Imperial Hotel in the early hours of Sunday Morning.

Worksop Station. Sunday, January 14th 2am.

Worksop supporters who could not afford to travel down to the match, stood in the freezing cold on platform one of the town's railway station eager to welcome home these working-class heroes and the travelling supporters when they got off the train from London, but there were no players to meet, only supporters. The supporters stepping off the train had heard that the players would not be travelling back with them, but other than rumours and speculation, they had nothing more to add.

The mood amongst the supporters as they walked or cycled home along frosty streets was one of disappointment and confusion, tempered by expectation. The worst-case scenario was that the directors would look for a bigger ground than Central Avenue. A replay in Sheffield or Nottingham on the following Thursday would draw the local sporting fraternity as well as 8 to 10,000 Worksop supporters. Little did they know that the directors had selected another option.

The Imperial Hotel. Sunday, January 14th 11am.

It was the events of Sunday that suggest that this was an unprecedented match switch, one that came with an itinerary to subvert and disable the threat of a team that had come inches away from humiliating Spurs on their own ground.

The Worksop players were themselves coy about what happened in the next 48 hours. They would spend two more nights in the plush Imperial Hotel, Russell Square. If the football club funded this stage of the adventure, then they did not record it in the club's minutes or accounts. There is no record of who paid for breakfast and dinner on the Sunday.

The nine miners - all the Worksop players in general - liked a drink and a smoke. As the Saturday night shenanigans showed, they were unlikely to turn down the offer of either, especially if someone else was picking up the 'tab.'

On Sunday morning, according to *The Nottingham Post*, the Worksop players as guests of the Tottenham club, embarked on a long and exhausting sight-seeing tour, with plenty of free alcohol and food provided. It was a great adventure, but the players, although powerless to intervene, would have been aware that it was a story that might make them appear complicit in the 'betrayal' back home.

18. Aftermath.

Clues as to the true story would emerge slowly. It was years before a few players admitted that they had been 'wined and dined' by the Tottenham directors and that they saw all the sites of London - whilst being generously looked after by their hosts. Drained by this experience and emotionally scarred by being denied the opportunity to return home as heroes, they were scarcely in a fit state to face Tottenham and Edmonton Cubs on the following Monday, let alone one of the finest teams in the land.

At the launch of a first volume of a history of Worksop Town in 2016, two members of Wilf Simmonite's family who attended, told Lance Hardy that the result of the second game had been 'fixed' but seemed reluctant to talk about it further, and despite entreaties, did not take the opportunity to converse again.

If there was a deal, then it must have been an extensive one.

Beloved and Betrayed

Many years later, during a debate on football governance in the House of Commons, former Bassetlaw MP John Mann, made an accusation of bribery against Spurs, backdated to 1923, to Tottenham MP David Lammy:

'In 1923, Tottenham Hotspur famously bribed Worksop Town to replay a match two days after its initial historic 0-0 draw, allegedly providing copious amounts of beer to disable the team.'

A presumably bewildered Lammy did not respond to Mann's specific allegation.

Could the triumvirate of Worksop directors have received what in later years came to become known as a bung, an unauthorised and undisclosed payment to a club manager - or any other decision-maker within a club? This practice had undoubtedly been a common feature of football for generations, most associated with sealing a transfer deal.

The Worksop players and directors would have been familiar with another slang term for an illicit payment, a 'back-hander.' According to the Merriam-Webster dictionary, this term was first used in 1803, originally in the context of a surprise punch or blow but later to describe a sly payment, a bribe, to secure a deal.

Could the Worksop directors have received cash in hand and then passed some of this on to the players to ensure their silence? Might this explain the players' reticence to talk about events after the first game beyond the occasional reference to 'being wined and dined' and 'enjoying the Spurs' tipple.' And might it also explain the 'fights' in the dressing room after the game before consensus was reached?

The evidence that corruption was institutionalised at all levels of football in the 1920's is compelling, and it extended beyond illegal financial transactions. The manipulation of promotions was well established and went on most years with teams being de-selected and replaced without a fair and consistent process.

The top northern and midland teams were not averse to effectively running a closed shop and blocking aspirational southern teams. The Football Association patriarchy also shamelessly suppressed the emerging women's game, banning them from using major stadiums because they were both alarmed at the size of the crowds they were attracting and the large subsequent charity donations.

Billy Meredith of Manchester City admitted that he, and others, tried to bribe Aston Villa players to secure a victory in 1905. A Good Friday 1915 game between Liverpool and Manchester United was fixed to save the latter from relegation. Seven players were initially banned for life. Phil Bratley, brother of Worksop player Horace played in this game, and was exonerated.

The Deal.

Were Tottenham Hotspur surprised by the quality of their visitors' performance and were they seriously worried that they could repeat the performance in the replay? There is evidence to suggest that they were troubled by the prospect of playing Worksop on their own ground. When the England international, former team captain and FA Cup winner, Tom Clay wrote his autobiography he found space to reflect on a distant footnote in his, and Tottenham Hotspurs' illustrious history. Speaking with commendable candour he admitted that Wally Amos had embarrassed him - 'One of the biggest run arounds I had during my career was against Wally Amos from a little mining village called Worksop.'

The Athletic News had not spared his blushes at the time, observing how Amos had 'flashed past him in most finished style.'

An astonished Spurs director was equally candid when speaking to a Worksop director. Monday, January 15th 1923 - 'By my word you're a tough lot, and as hard as steel.'

The Westminster Gazette was scathing about Spurs performance, claiming that their strikers were 'dead scared they were not going to win.'

The game is still remembered, by the hard core of Spurs' supporters who are interested in the minutiae of the club's history, as a memorably uncomfortable occasion. The Hotspur.com website concludes: 'What an embarrassment this was for Tottenham.' Reflecting on how it was 'unthinkable that Spurs should stumble against humble Worksop.'

Jimmy Seed was another Tottenham star who carried the memory of the game with him for the rest of his career. Lance Hardy had the opportunity to look at the future Charlton managers 'book of drawings and formations.' In his 28-year managerial career, Seed always selected a centre-half at the heart of his defence. The first time he played against this system was during the cup tie against Worksop. As a manager, he also routinely mentioned the game to focus the mind of his players before FA Cup games.

The stakes were high - it was deemed essential by Tottenham's directors and supporters that, to retain their London pre-eminence, they should be the first London team to lift the FA Cup at Wembley.

Worksop supporters, then and now, rationally assessing the performance at White Hart Lane, with a team short of three of their best players, in an intimidating atmosphere – and at one of the most iconic stadiums in Britain, believed that Worksop Town would have had an outstanding chance of beating Tottenham Hotspur at Central Avenue.

Taking Chance Out of the Equation.

The available evidence suggests that there was a desire amongst the Spurs chairman and directors to leave nothing to chance. They clearly had the financial means to ensure that Spurs would progress smoothly to the next round and erase the shameful embarrassment of the first game by administering a comprehensive thrashing to the Tigers from Worksop. What followed was a project, a complex strategic deal. It went much further than simply negotiating a ground switch for the replay.

The practice of offering money to switch venues and buy home advantage was as old as the hills. Technically it was against FA regulations, FA Cup rule 12 stating that 'No monetary or other consideration shall be asked for or paid in connection with negotiation for a change of venue.' But there was no established protocol for investigation, no likelihood of punishment and therefore no incentive to stay on the right side of the law.

It is hard not to feel some sympathy for the three directors who made the decision - they had plenty to worry about. Worksop FC had been on a precarious ride from the start, teetering on the precipice of oblivion several times in each decade, the complex web of the club's finances

Beloved and Betrayed

stabilised by archery tournaments, a troop of minstrels, smoking concerts and the patronage of the Dukes and Duchesses of Portland and Newcastle, and, more occasionally, prudent financial management by directors who were characteristically self-made men, new to the middle class.

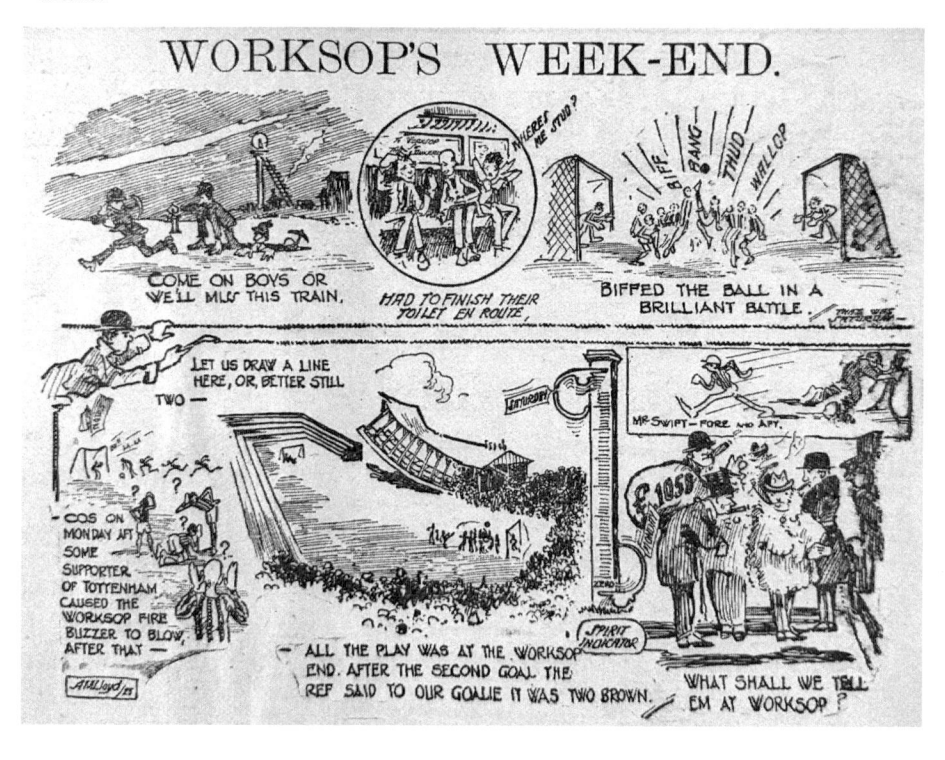

Sunday Pictorial, Tottenham Hotspur v Worksop Town (SP

19. Tottenham Hotspur v Worksop Town (replay).
White Hart Lane. Monday, January 15th. 2.30pm

The replay was a farce. There was only a thin scattering of Worksop supporters in the ground. Only a few would have been able to afford the additional costs and the travelling supporters were too angry with the directors perceived betrayal to stick around anyway. As one said, 'The never-failing, rain or shine, win or lose spectators are deprived of their right to see the Spurs.'

'Money, money all the time' said another in a letter to *The Worksop Guardian*. It was 'not the way to treat people who had lost a day's work and travelled to London to give the team their moral and financial support.'

From the kick-off it was clear that Worksop Town were only a shadow of the team that had put up such a spirited performance just two days earlier. It might have been different had they been awarded what appeared to be a certain penalty in the opening minutes, after Lilley was blatantly bowled over in the penalty area. At least one Spurs' director was embarrassed by the referee's decision.

A Spurs penalty swiftly followed, which Brown saved. The Worksop players looked exhausted. They played like men who had nothing left to give. Worksop had demonstrated their fitness in the first game. Unfortunately, we will never know whether the Worksop players, after a few days rest and recuperation, would have been fully competitive again on the following Thursday. That possibility had been taken care of.

From then on Spurs attacked with arrogant impunity and Worksop showed little resistance. Inside-left Charles Handley sailed through, scarcely challenged and opened the scoring on fifteen minutes.

After this, Worksop were swept aside with four goals in eight minutes. Lindsay scored two and Seed added a fourth before Handley delivered his second. The Worksop team looked drained and exhausted.

In the second half, Handley secured his hat-trick and goals from Dimmock, and Lindsay, took the total to nine.

As Tommy Lawrie, would admit after joking poker-faced about 'nine breakaways' they had 'enjoyed the Spurs tipple' too much, and anyway, what was there to fight for? If they achieved the impossible and forced another replay, it would be at White Hart Lane anyway.

The nine goals conceded could have been 19 were it not for the heroics of Jack Brown, fighting desperately against an unjust stain on his career. His performance was inspirational, the rest played like men whose hearts had been broken.

Beloved and Betrayed

Back home in Worksop the result was a bigger shock than the first. The 9-0 defeat was greeted with a mixture of disgust and incredulity. Fans knew that, in normal circumstances, the team were incapable of being beaten by such a margin. The supporter's bitterness and cold fury increased. They had already decided who was to blame and it was not the players or Tottenham Hotspur Football Club.

Whilst the game was taking place the draw for the Second Round of the FA Cup was made. Had Worksop beaten Spurs in the replay they would have faced Manchester United at home in the next round.

Daily Mail cartoon, the replay, 1923 (DM)

Homeward Bound. Monday, January 15th 7pm.

Chairman Tomlinson appeared to be in a world of his own.

'We are all going home delighted with ourselves.' Tomlinson announced at London's Kings Cross railway station to reporters, after the humiliating 9-0 trouncing, showing off a pretty cheque for £2,865 in gate money from the two matches. It had a nice picture of White Hart Lane printed on top.

The coverage in the national newspapers quickly switched from praise to ridicule after a hapless performance. A cartoon in *The Daily Mail* sarcastically suggested that the reason for the replay and the heavy defeat was that the players wanted to get back to work as soon as possible. They were 'missing their old Davy Lamp' and 'Pit Mouth.'

The Monday afternoon replay, although a working day, drew a crowd of 23,122. At least exiled Worksopians in Christchurch, New Zealand, were happy, the local paper carried a report on a shock 9-0 win for Worksop in the replay!

Waiting on Worksop station was a welcoming party for the players (who were, quite rightly, greeted as heroes) There were pantomime boos and jeers for the directors: as they stepped off the train they were greeted with an orchestrated chant, 'Up with the players, down, with the directors.'

20. The Game that Might Have Been.

Hindsight is a wonderful thing, but the decision to stop the story of that game at White Hart Lane, rather than on the moist and muddy turf of Central Avenue means that we will never know how the adventure might have ended.

If finance (legal or otherwise) had been the motive for the Worksop directors' decision there is no evidence (in either the club's accounts or minutes) to suggest that any additional fees, other than gate money were received. This seems odd given that the same Worksop chairman had struck a deal with another London First Division club when selling ground rights some fifteen years earlier.

A home replay on the following Thursday, which was a half-day holiday in Worksop, would have seen the team fresh and recovered. In addition, both the absent 'Tommys' - best player Spink and top scorer Cawley - may both have been available.

The unprecedented outpouring of anger and frustration that greeted the decision to switch the tie did not simply reflect the loss of a good day out and a memorable adventure for the players and supporters of Worksop Town. It was born out of faith, a belief in an exceptional group of men having the potential to achieve something unprecedented and extraordinary. Neither players nor supporters were astonished by the result of the first game because they knew that this was no ordinary Worksop Town outfit, it was a team that had the elusive, almost indefinable quality later espoused by Tom Wolfe in 1979 in '*The Right Stuff*.' The ambition, self-belief and courage necessary for success. They also sensed that this was the defining moment in the club's history, and that they would never see the like again.

The directors chose to blame drawn games delivering three replays in Sheffield and Nottingham. Chairman Tomlinson said, 'Three cup ties in six days in Sheffield and Nottingham was too much of a good thing.'

This was unconvincing. The visit of Tottenham Hotspur to Central Avenue would have been a standout tie, a game that would have elicited enthusiasm across the whole of the United Kingdom. A big crowd would have been a certainty.

They also blamed the size of the ground. Central Avenue had a capacity of 8,000. This point had some validity, but supporters would have accepted a significant price hike for such a unique event and there was a fighting chance of a money-spinning draw in the next round if they won.

The directors later stated that they had deliberated for an hour before making the decision and claimed that they had previously contacted both Sheffield clubs to ascertain whether they would have been willing to host the replay. If they did, there is no record of any phone calls or correspondence. Neither Sheffield club has any records of a discussion.

We know that the directors believed that the team could obtain a positive result at White Hart Lane suggesting that a deal and a switch was always their intention, if Worksop shocked Spurs. If the Worksop supporters found this unfathomable and unforgivable, they viewed the directors' decision to sanction the playing of the game two days later, either an act of exceptional stupidity or confirmation that the officials had been 'bought' and 'were lining their own pockets.'

The directors would spend the weeks and months after the game - the ones who lived in the town, the rest of their lives - defending their decision. The decision to then blame the supporters was as foolish a mistake, from their perspective, as the one to agree to switch the replay. They argued that the crowds had been 'disappointing' and 'inadequate,' forcing the directors to make the tough but realistic decision to sacrifice cup glory to save the club from liquidation. *The Worksop Guardian* supported the director's decision whole heartedly:

"Poor gates, had the position been healthy the directors would not have hesitated for one minute' (to bring Spurs to Worksop.)

'Money isn't everything, the directors know that.'

Suggesting, without intended irony, that instead of boycotting the games the directors, supporters and players should 'hang together.'

This was also nonsense, per head of population, Worksop's average crowd of between 3 and 4,000 was remarkable given the size of the town. As we have seen, the supporters club was a well organised machine with a constant stream of money pouring into the club -enough to build offices and dressing rooms without troubling the directors for a contribution. The club minutes prior to the game express the usual concerns without suggesting that a serious fiscal crisis was looming.

Most of the national, and regional papers inevitably backed the directors, *The Daily Despatch* ran with the headline, 'Cup Lost but Club Saved' - a neat summary that was picked up by many other newspapers. There was little space for the opinions of the working man in the press of that era, but there were dissenting voices. Predictably the liberal *Manchester Guardian* was the most condemnatory.

'This arrangement seems to be against the rule prohibiting the sale of a club's right to play at home. Sale it must be for although Tottenham may not have promised any definite sum of money the game has not been taken to Worksop.' It was 'another sacrifice to filthy lucre.'

The Sheffield Star observed that: 'Many a time the pure course of football has been befouled by this bartering of rights.'

Until recent times, every son and daughter of a Worksop Town supporter was told the story of the great betrayal, almost as a 'rite-of-passage' into the world of grown-up football. The parents, in turn, had been given the story from their own fathers. Many supporters, especially the ones who had endured the switching of the Chelsea tie in 1908, orchestrated by two of the same directors, vowed that they would never watch the club again. *The Worksop Guardian*, whilst defending the director's decision published some of the condemnatory letters.

The board launched a PR exercise and Tom Richardson was instructed, as captain, to 'hang together' and defend the indefensible. The letter following the acrimonious fall-out from the replay, claimed that all the Worksop players had been in full agreement with the director's decision to switch home advantage. It reminded the players that the 'directors have always treated players 'in a most gentlemanly manner' and 'that wages were always paid.' This was a fair point; the club had been professionally run since the end of the war, and there was plenty of affection shown by the directors towards 'our boys.' It also stated that directors paid their own expenses.

Whether Tom Richardson wrote the letter, or simply signed it, is unclear. The idea that the players were happy to see the opportunity to have their family and friends greet them as local heroes at the biggest home game in Worksop's history, only to have potential immortality seemingly snatched away from them, is ludicrous. In 1923 footballers were expected to know their place - they would have been aware that all but one of the dissenting voices in 1919 were swiftly removed from the club.

Lance Hardy interviewed Tom Richardson's son, Alan, who is no longer with us. He said that his father told him that, although he carried on playing - 'I was finished with football from that day forward.'

In retrospect, whether the directors lined their own pockets or simply tried to do the right thing for the long-term future of the club, the switch was undoubtedly a horrible mistake. Worksop had a once-in-a-football-lifetime opportunity to reserve their place in the annals of football history -and they blew it. Something in the club was broken, and it

Beloved and Betrayed

would take generations before the bond between the club and its supporters was to be restored.

Hanging Together.

Although a hard core of the 'betrayed' supporters kept their pledge, and a long-term trend of attendance decline was established, inevitably many Worksop Town supporters drifted back to what was in some cases their only recreational activity. The team settled back into the league routine and resumed their winning ways, for the rest of January. The superb home run continued through February and the first half of March.

On Thursday March 15th 1923, Denaby United beat the Tigers 1-0 and, in so doing, became the first team to defeat Worksop at Central Avenue for two years! The Tigers took out their frustration at losing this proud record by thrashing Rotherham Town 6-0 in their next game. On April 3rd (Easter Monday) *The Sheffield Independent* remarked on the chaos at Sheffield Victoria station, as Liverpool fans arriving for their game at Bramall Lane mingled with Worksop fans heading to Hillsborough.

Two goals from Cawley and a strike from Rippon secured the points against Forest Reserves, in front of 2,000. Scunthorpe succumbed by the same margin in the next home game, Rippon, Spink, and Cawley doing the damage. The game against York was more frantic and open, the Tigers eventually prevailing by 5-3.

An end of season third place behind Wednesday Reserves and Doncaster Rovers represented a creditable effort. The reserves also won the Mansfield Charity Cup and the Sheffield Association League. They had surpassed the efforts of the old rivals Mansfield Town and Rotherham Town and they were ahead of York City and Scunthorpe United - despite the advantages of size and population enjoyed by the future league clubs.

21. The Road to Wembley.

Tottenham Hotspur, with their pride restored after a crushing victory in the replay, consigned Worksop Town to a historical footnote and swiftly recovered their composure, putting six goals past Oldham Athletic in back-to-back games. Grimsdell had whetted his appetite for attacking forays, joining Lindsay and Dimmock on the scoresheet at Oldham. In the home game Clay scored two penalties and Lindsay added a third without reply.

On February 3rd 1923, the road to Wembley re-opened with a home game against Manchester United, in the Second Round, the equivalent of the Fourth Round today, a place in the last 16 beckoning. In glorious sunshine a crowd of 38,333 saw Spurs completely outclass Manchester United - *The Sunday Post* reporting that Spurs were 'superior in every department.' Lindsay was in devastating form, tormenting the Manchester United defence from the start, scoring a fine first goal and feeding Handley with sublimely timed passes. Handley went on to score three more and only a tremendous performance from the Manchester United keeper Mew, stopped Spurs from winning by a margin of six or seven goals.

The First Division campaign was less satisfactory. Liverpool were heading for back-to-back titles while Spurs, unable to build on their runners-up spot from the previous season, slipped to mid-table, destined to finish in 12th place, one below Arsenal. The quest for Wembley glory was the top priority. But Spurs' luck ran out when the draw for the Third Round brought an away game. Spurs would face a difficult trip to Wales to face Cardiff City on February 24th.

Out of the teams left in the last 16 of the competition, Tottenham were favoured by many, alongside Huddersfield Town, the previous year's winners. Huddersfield were one of a quartet of Yorkshire clubs still standing, alongside both Sheffield teams and Barnsley. The champions, and league leaders, Liverpool, yet to lift the trophy, had a home draw against Sheffield United.

Liverpool's season tended to be defined by their quest for the FA Cup. Even two league titles in succession could not compensate for failure in the greatest competition of all. Three more London clubs, West Ham United, Charlton Athletic and Queens Park Rangers, were also dreaming of a day of glory at the Empire Stadium, as were Tottenham's old Southern League rivals Southampton.

On a wretched surface in front of a crowd of 55,000 at Ninian Park, Spurs expected a tough challenge. Clay was left out, Grimsdell dropping back to full-back, with Skinner taking his place in the half-back line.

Beloved and Betrayed

They started brightly with slick passing moves between Seed and Walden and soon put the Cardiff goal under pressure. Cardiff's cause was not helped when they conceded a silly goal, a mistake by Blair being pounced upon by Lindsay who was on a fine run of form. The hapless Blair was responsible for the second goal too, Seed charging down his clearance. His subsequent hand ball leading to a free-kick, which Seed converted with ease.

Lindsay's third would prove to be the decisive strike of the game. It was just as well that Spurs established a three-goal lead because Cardiff came surging back in the second half, scoring twice. Only a commanding performance from the England skipper Grimsdell kept Spurs on the road to Wembley.

With the emerging northern powerhouse Huddersfield Town knocked out by lowly Bolton Wanderers, Sheffield United adding to Liverpool's dismal cup record by dismissing the league leaders at Anfield, and West Bromwich Albion humbled by Second Division Charlton Athletic, there were no representatives from the top eight of the First Division left in the competition. It all seemed set fair for 'the Darlings of Fortune' when Spurs, once again, secured home advantage at the Quarter-Final stage.

Disaster followed. Coached by the legendary figure of Steve Bloomer, Derby County delivered the FA Cup shock that Worksop Town had come close to achieving two months earlier. In front of 50,349 spectators, they attacked Spurs from the start. Grimsdell set the tone, the remarkably consistent Spurs skipper appearing to panic under pressure, heading backwards towards his own goal. The crowd were alarmed. Derby had noted the success of Amos and Cammack against the Spurs full-backs during the Worksop tie, and Clay had a nightmare being consistently outpaced by Murphy. Spurs created more chances than they had against Worksop but were profligate in front of goal. In retrospect the 1-0 defeat, billed as a major shock, was a significant turning point in the history of Tottenham Hotspur.

In April West Ham United would be the London club to contest the first Wembley FA Cup Final, a game which has become known as 'the White Horse Final' after the horse that helped clear the pitch of fans. Although West Ham looked likely winners at first, Bolton grew in strength and dominated the match - David Jack scoring the first and Jack Smith adding a controversial second goal during the second half.

22. A third betrayal and an unlikely reunion.

Jack and Jimmy save the Owls.

An old proverb says, 'It's an ill wind that blows no good.' Jack Brown, who scarcely had a shot to save in the first game at White Hart Lane but nevertheless kept a clean sheet, would have his life transformed not by the blast of nine goals tearing past him in the catastrophic second game, but by the shots that he kept out. The Wednesday had been keeping an eye on Jack. He was already considered to be the best goal-keeper in the Midland League, and his performance in saving his demoralised, over-walked, over-fed and hungover colleagues from an even greater humiliation, clinched the deal.

Brown was purchased by Wednesday as a back up to their England goalkeeper Teddy Davison, who was coming to the end of his career. He was transferred to Hillsborough on February 23rd 1923 for a £360 fee. At 24, Jack Brown was approaching his peak as a goal keeper and was about to realise his full potential in a rapid surge to the pinnacle of the professional game.

It took time for Brown, who was a reluctant goalkeeper and footballer anyway, to settle in, and he was almost released by The Wednesday before an arm-break for Davison gave him his opportunity. He eventually made the position his own during the 1925/26 campaign, when Wednesday were promoted to the First Division as Second Division Champions, with Brown keeping a sensational 16 clean sheets.

In the same season, Jimmy Seed sustained what was perceived to be a career-threatening ankle injury. For the second time in his career, he was treated with humiliating and infuriating contempt by his employers. The man who had been the both the engine room and the creative inspiration of the Spurs midfield was written off as a 'crock' as manager Billy Minter decided to replace him with a talented youngster and player with a name that would have been a perfect fit for Roy of the Rovers, Taffy O'Callaghan.

Seed was demoted and left to lick his wounds in the Spurs' reserves, where, to add insult to injury, he would also face a pay cut. It was another example of the master-servant relationship that defined the lives of professional footballers in this era and made talented players like Jack Brown and Tommy Lawrie reluctant to leave the financial security of coal mining, for a career that could end abruptly with one rash challenge.

Seed decided to take charge of his own destiny and become a 'master' himself by accepting a managerial role at Aldershot. However, when the Wednesday the made an offer for his services in 1927, Tottenham decided that they would block Aldershot and give Seed 'Hobson's Choice' - a wage cut and a spell kicking his talented heels in 'the stiffs,' or a move back north.

In another twist of fate, Arthur Lowdell, the player that Peter McWilliam had been watching at Mid-Rhondda when he spotted Jimmy Seed, would finally arrive at Tottenham and Seed would be reacquainted with Jack Brown.

Taffy O'Callaghan was a decent player. Born in Ebbw Vale, Wales, he joined Tottenham from Ebbw Vale FC in 1925, making his debut for the first team in January 1927 against Everton. Taffy had natural balance and was two-footed, he could also play the 'pass and move' game that was already part of Tottenham Hotspur's footballing DNA. Lowdell was also a decent player who would go on to make 90 appearances for Spurs and become club captain.

O'Callaghan helped the team achieve promotion back to the Football League First Division at the end of the 1932/33 season. During his time at Spurs, he made 252 league appearances scoring 93 goals and a further six in 11 FA Cup matches for the club. However, Seed was the man who had commanded the Spurs midfield by instinct and intellect. He was irreplaceable.

Up the Owls.

For once karma or natural justice would prevail and Billy Minter would live to regret his contemptible lack of respect for the Spurs' legend. Initially it was Seed who felt like he had been tossed from frying pan to fire. The Wednesday were newly promoted and struggling in the top flight, well below their neighbours, the 1925 FA Cup winners Sheffield United. They were also below Spurs. At the end of March 1927, Wednesday were certainties for relegation, having won just two of their previous 15 games. The newspapers decided they were a lost cause. Bob Brown the Wednesday manager was a north-easterner like Seed, and it was not long before the senior professional Seed was installed as club captain. It was a wise choice.

Despite his knee injury Seed could still use his positional sense and tactical knowledge to orchestrate attacks, and, as skipper, he could advise younger players and improve tactical awareness throughout the squad. Ellis Rimmer bought from Tranmere Rovers, proved to be an inspirational signing, as Seed and Rimmer, supported by the sure hands of Jack Brown, inspired one of football's greatest escape stories. The Wednesday secured a remarkable 17 points out of a possible 20 in the last ten matches and avoided relegation by a point. More irony followed. Wednesday's remarkable recovery sent Spurs tumbling into the Second Division.

Tottenham were a little unlucky, relegated with 38 points, a record for a relegated club in the era of two points for a win. Seed scored in both games against Spurs, at Hillsborough and White Hart Lane. Whilst lamenting his old club's bad luck, Seed could be forgiven if he took quiet satisfaction, even 'Schadenfreude' at effectively ending the career of the manager who had treated him so shabbily.

Minter's Spurs struggled in the Second Division, finishing tenth in the 1928/29 season. During the 1929/30 season Minter resigned due to failing health, brought on by stress. He blamed his stress on his failure at the club to which he was undoubtedly devoted too, and reflected on his decision to sell Seed. In *Tottenham Hotspur the Complete Record*, Bob Goodwin states that the decision to sell Seed 'must rank alongside the departure of Pat Jennings as one of the worst made by Spurs.' Tottenham Hotspur would spend the next five years in the Second Division, whilst Sheffield Wednesday, with Jimmy Seed as captain and Jack Brown in goal, slipped out of Sheffield United's shadow to win back-to-back First Division titles.

23. If Only We'd had Spink. Part Two.

As the Roaring Twenties reached the middle year of the decade, Worksop Town were enduring death by a thousand cuts. The spine of the 1922 Midland League Championship team had been broken with the irreplaceable Jack Brown moving to The Wednesday, the Froggatt brothers heading to Gainsborough Trinity, and the irrepressible Tommy Lawrie moving between Mansfield Town and Gainsborough Trinity.

Tommy would collect two more Midland League Championship medals before returning to the Manton Colliery team. Wally Amos was off to Bury where he would become a club legend, and their second all-time highest goal scorer. A significant minority continued their boycott of home games and the bond of trust between players, supporters and directors had been further eroded by the Spurs debacle. If this was not enough for the club to endure, a series of bitter industrial disputes and the ensuing 1926 General Strike, damaged the club irrevocably.

The Tigers slipped to fourth place in the Midland League in 1924/25 when Notts rivals Mansfield and Tommy Lawrie were crowned champions and finished mid-table in 1925/26 when Mexborough were 'kings' of the Midland League. However, there was to be one last moment of glory for the remaining cup fighting heroes of 1923, Tom Richardson, and George Robinson.

Worksop faced a tricky start to their FA Cup campaign, though once again exempt to the Fourth Qualifying Round, they were then drawn away at Newark. On this occasion, the Tigers managed to overcome their old cup rivals and secure a home draw against an emerging force in Coventry City of the Third Division North. City, formed from the Singer Sewing Machine company, were destined to win the FA Cup, but that was many years hence.

The Town directors, still suffering from the fall-out from the Spurs game, stated that the game would be played at Central Avenue and that there 'was no point' in Coventry entreating them to switch the tie, as they would not give the suggestion, 'their slightest consideration.' Whether it was a bluff to entice more money, the game was destined to be played in Worksop.

Beloved and Betrayed

The four days of fame that Worksop had enjoyed in the capital swiftly dissipated. They were non-entities once more - one London paper stating that they were a 'mining village in Cumberland' on several occasions (*Coventry Evening Telegraph* November 25th 1925).

But Tom Richardson had not lost his faith in his team.

'As soon as I knew the draw, I said it was a good one.'

On a frost-bound, heavily sanded pitch covered in light snow, Coventry were at full strength whilst Worksop were missing striker Albert Rawson who had fractured his rib two weeks earlier. Both teams had goalkeepers called Best on the pitch, Jerry for Coventry and George Best, the Tiger's custodian.

Worksop Town

1 G Best

2 Hunt   5 Robinson   3 Richardson

4 Tuffnell   6 Challoner

8 Binney   10 A A Shelley

7 Spink   9 Tremelling   11 Bluff

Coventry City

1 J Best

2 Cahouldy   3 Randle

4 McAlvaney   5 Watson   6 Rowley

8 Turner   10 Herbert

7 Dongall   9 Phereson   11 Walker

The players wearing crêpe armlets in tribute to the late Queen Alexandra observed a minute's silence before kick-off. Coventry looked uncomfortable in the initial stages. Although they won the toss, Coventry elected to face the sun, which troubled them, as did an aggressive and focused Worksop side and the notoriously variable, Central Avenue pitch. George Robinson sent Tommy Spink tearing down the right.

Spink sent a perfect cross hurtling into the penalty area and Coventry had a narrow escape as Tremelling hit the upright. *The Sheffield Star* recorded how Spink and Binney made the Coventry defence look small. At the back, George Robinson was as dominant as he had been against Spurs two years earlier, marshalling his defence and launching an attack which saw a brilliant Binney shot tipped away by Jerry Best.

Worksop were cheered off after a superb first-half display which had clearly rattled a complacent Coventry side. *The Sheffield Star* reflected on Richardson's supreme coolness and noted he was 'energetic to the last ounce.'

The old warrior Richardson made a critical intervention as Coventry rallied at the start of the second half, Patterson being dispossessed by a sublimely timed tackle. Coventry went long and direct to counter Worksop's pass and move service to Binney and Spink on the right. Suddenly they were back in the game, creating a flurry of chances. Herbert hit the upright and Turner another post when it would have been easier to score.

In a fast, open, and exciting second half, Worksop Town created chances, and Tremelling and Binney both squandered them. The decisive moment in the game came when, with Worksop's Shelley already on the floor injured, the Coventry keeper collided with Bluff and both players crashed to the floor, hitting the frozen surface hard. As Binney headed the ball into the apparently empty net, a Coventry player Randle appeared and punched the ball away with both fists. The crowd roared and the referee pointed to the spot without hesitation.

4,630 fans fell silent as Spink stepped up to take the kick. With ice in his veins, the experienced pro approached the ball confidently and delivered one of the best giant-killing results in the club's history. It was one of Central Avenue's finest moments and remains an embarrassing footnote in Coventry's story. *The Coventry Evening Telegraph* describing it as, a 'tragic 90 minutes' their 'most inglorious failure in post-war football' whilst damning Worksop with faint praise. The Tigers were 'plucky' and a 'determined, hard-working defensive side.' Ruefully a Coventry director reflected on Worksop's 'twelfth man.'

'Never on a football field have I ever seen such wild excitement.' He went on to describe a spectator, 'vaulting from the grandstand, tearing the midfield touchline flag from the ground and waving it riotously around his head.'

For many supporters though it was a reminder of what might have been. The 1923 team had been significantly stronger than the 1925 team, even missing the talisman, Spink. Worksop had beaten a team that would go on to lift the FA Cup, they would do the same again on two occasions (beating Bradford City and Wigan Athletic) but a victory over Spurs would have trumped the lot. It did nothing to erase the bitterness felt by their estranged supporters.

There was a time when their next opponents Third Division Chesterfield would have been pessimistic about a visit to Worksop, regardless of the status of the two teams. For many years Central Avenue was their ultimate bogey ground and the Tigers their nemesis. However, cup triumph on their last visit had exorcised the ghosts of previous defeats and they had enough skill and professionalism, to prevail by 2-1. Had the Tigers progressed they would have faced Orient in the next round. A crowd of 8,171, still a record, was some consolation.

24. Oblivion.

There can be no doubt that the decision to switch the Spurs game was a catastrophic and irredeemable mistake and one that changed the destiny of Worksop Town Football Club. Although crowds still turned out for big games, an atmosphere of bitterness and mistrust remained for decades between the directors and supporters. Exacerbated by further Industrial conflicts, average crowds and revenue plummeted. In 1929 the team that had been the golden boys in the first five years of the decade finished bottom and, a year later, they went into liquidation.

Although the town club rose, phoenix-like, from the ashes a few days later it was not until the 1950's that the spirit of the club really revived.

What Became of the Likely Lads?

Although none of the 'Boys of '23' went on to emulate Jack Brown's international career, most did achieve further footballing success. Tom

Richardson stayed loyal to his home town club and Manton Colliery, earning a well-supported and lucrative benefit season which ended with a game against Rotherham Amateurs. He passed away in the 1970's. His defensive partner, Horace Bratley, close to the end of his career, moved back to his native Rawmarsh, near Rotherham.

Of the half-backs, Wilf Simmonite, the clerk, stayed for another season and was selected for the Midland League Representative side against the champions in 1924. George Robinson played local football and continued working as a miner. He was destined for a tragic end, crushed and killed in an accident with coal tubs in the 1940's.

Both Froggatts swiftly went on to pastures new, winning the Midland League with Gainsborough Trinity and having successful cricket careers in the Bassetlaw league. They continued to live in the pretty Yorkshire village of Harthill and their pub, the Blue Bell, became a focal point for ex-players to talk about old times and reflect on how their lives might have changed had Worksop brought Tottenham Hotspur back to Central Avenue.

Of the five forwards, right-winger Frankie Cammack remained with the club, although never producing a performance better than his remarkable and unexpected cameo at White Hart Lane. Wally Amos, the player who caused Spurs huge problems, whilst not quite reaching the dizzy heights of Jack Brown, also used his remarkable afternoon as a stepping stone to footballing immortality signing for Bury, in the summer of 1923 becoming a stalwart and ever-present member of the team that won promotion to the top flight.

In 1926 *The Green 'Un* described him as one of the 'pluckiest fellows who ever kicked a ball.' Whenever Amos played in Sheffield, hundreds of Worksop supporters would travel to watch him play. As late as 1932 *The Sheffield Independent* was describing the 'dapper little chap' as the 'danger man' of the Bury attack.

The Liverpool Echo, December 7th 1945, congratulating Bury on their 60th anniversary, described Wally as 'their greatest ever player.' An exceptional accolade given that Bury had previously won the FA Cup on two occasions. Despite playing most of his career as a winger Amos is Bury's third highest goal scorer of all time, with 122 goals.

Beloved and Betrayed

Wally's finest achievement was selection for a Football League side that played the Irish League in 1926. He finished his career at Accrington Stanley in 1935 and passed away in 1967. He was 68 years old. In interviews he often talked about the quality of the Worksop Town team of 1923.

Bill Lilley chose to remain with the Tigers, 28 in 1923 he aged gracefully and assisted the reserves in his thirties, dying at the age of 71 in 1964. The affection of the Worksop supporters for 'Old Bill' was immense and it is no coincidence that, amongst the few surviving artefacts from Worksop Town in this era, are a number of decorated match-boxes in the Tigers colours with Bill's picture on one side and the 1923 squad on the other, sold to raise money for his testimonial.

'Pip' Rippon, at 34 years of age, was coming to the end of an extensive career in 1923. He left Worksop that year and had spells with three other Midland League clubs, York City, Wath Athletic and Grantham. He died in 1950, aged 62.

Tommy Lawrie would also leave Worksop Town that summer, seduced by a 'golden hello' from Mansfield Town. One of the best players in the Midland League for a decade, he would go on to turn down offers to join the Football League, because he knew he could earn more by combining mining and football. He remained a Manton miner, moving to surface work in the 1940s. Lawrie subsequently became the only player to win three Midland League titles with three different clubs: Worksop Town (1922) Mansfield Town (1924) and Gainsborough Trinity (1928). He was with Mansfield when they won a place in Division Three North.

A keen cyclist he climbed on his bike and rode over to local firm Carlton Cycles to work two days a week and managed to stay active well into his 80's, before passing away in his home town of Worksop where he lived with his daughter and family. In 1976 he was interviewed in *The Worksop Guardian*, as the last survivor of the 'Boys of '23.'

The two other players unlucky enough to miss the game both stayed with the club the following season. Thomas Cawley joined Wilf Simmonite in the Midland League Representative team that played against the Midland League Champions Mansfield in 1924. He later played for Scunthorpe United, dying at the age of 89 in 1980.

Tommy Spink, the hero of Worksop's giant-killing victory over Coventry City, was rewarded with a lucrative benefit game in 1927 against Grimsby Town. He moved to Cleethorpes with his family after finishing his footballing career, managing a tobacconist shop prior to his retirement. He died in Cleethorpes in 1966.

The Long and Winding Road.

It took decades for the Worksop football club to re-awaken its bond with its supporters and with the town. The Spurs game left a legacy of mistrust and bitterness that lingered for over a generation. It was only when the club finally managed to be re-elected to the Midland League in 1949, after a gap of almost 20 years, that the club began to find its feet again at a level acceptable to its long-suffering supporters. In 1956 the Tigers reached the Third Round of FA Cup (last 64) beating ex-FA Cup winners Bradford City 1-0 at Central Avenue, in front of a crowd of 6,184, before losing 0-1 at Swindon.

In 1961 Worksop had another encouraging cup run, reaching the First Round Proper of FA Cup losing 0-2 at Workington, but it was not until 1966, the World Cup winning year, that they had another team that elicited almost as much love and affection as the 'Boys of '23.'

This team was based on attack not defence and was arguably more exciting to watch than the team which won the Midland League in 1922. In defiance of fashion and science they ignored the by then dominant 4-4-2 and retained an attacking line of five with two wingers. Throwing caution to the wind they attacked every team in the Midland League with gusto and conceded almost as many goals as they scored.

In winning the Midland League for the first time since 1922 they accrued a sensational 155 goals in only 34 games and several crowds topped 2,000 in a seasonal average of 1,755. Whilst significantly below the Central Avenue crowds of the 1920's, the average was indicative of a return of trust.

The Lord Mayor Alf Burton and his colleagues unequivocally decided to make the most of this moment in the town's history with a civic reception. A 'brand-new, luxury motor-coach' would depart from Central Avenue and journey slowly through the town, arriving at the Town Hall to be met by distinguished guests. Other vehicles were invited to join the procession, and some accepted the invitation. Supporters who were there recall one lorry, in an echo of events of 1922, carrying an almost life-sized toy Tiger.

Outside the Town Hall, young Tigers' supporters, sporting black and amber rosettes and waving rattles stood alongside grandparents who had waited forlornly on Worksop station in 1923. They chanted 'Ti-gers' 'Ti-gers' separated by four swift claps, in the fashion of the day, as skipper Dennis Lunn lifted the championship trophy to wild cheers and high-pitched squeals of delight.

25. Immortal Memory.

The Lord Mayor declared it 'the greatest event in the club's history' pausing briefly before adding, 'The present feat has done much to eliminate the memory of what happened at - and after - White Hart Lane.'

And then something magical happened. The 'Boys of '66' smartly attired in their blue blazers adorned with the Worksop coat of arms savoured their moment as the most entertaining and free-scoring side in the club's history. There were especially loud cheers for the local lads, John Harrison and David Howard, who milked the applause. The attacking triumvirate of Alan Vest, Ken Bell and Paul Leadbeater also received a unique ovation.

With proceedings almost over and the crowd beginning to think about travelling home, the Lord Mayor surprised everyone by calling upon four other footballers to move centre stage to receive the approbation of the crowd. At first there was confusion, the entire squad and management team had taken a bow, who was left to be lauded ? But then, as the last four survivors of the Worksop Town team of 1923: Tom Richardson, Tommy Lawrie, and the two Froggatt brothers hesitantly climbed the steps and were recognised by the crowd, there was a remarkable cheer that exceeded any that had gone before.

As they stood with tears in their eyes, bewildered by the warmth of the affection, 43 years on, they realised that 'Boys of '23' had not been forgotten. That four-decade gap has now stretched to a century and, as we record their names in this book, we know that, in Worksop at least, they will live in immortal memory.

Their story is part of Lance Hardy's legacy too. Alongside his fine book, '*Stokoe, Sunderland and '73*', acknowledged as the definitive book about the greatest day in the history of his equally beloved professional football club, this was the other great romantic football story that he knew was destined to carry his name.

As George Eliot once said, 'Our dead are never dead to us, until we have forgotten them.'

Years later, Terry Pratchett, another writer who sadly also died far too young, expressed it more poetically:

'No one is finally dead until the ripples they cause in the world die away, until the clock wound up winds down, until the wine she made has finished its ferment, until the crop they planted is harvested. The span of someone's life is only the core of their actual existence.'

References and Further Reading

Cameron, J. (1908), '*Association Football and How to Play it.*' Reprinted 2017. Create Space Independent Publishing Platform. ISBN: 978-1542721110

Hardy, L. (2011), *Stokoe, Sunderland and 73: The Story of the Greatest FA Cup Final Shock of All Time*. Orion. ISBN: 8601406997141

'Hotspurhq' website: https://hotspurhq.com/2014/01/13/tottenham-day-two-fa-cup-ties-non-league-opponents/

Lamming, D. (1985), '*A Who's Who of Grimsby Town AFC 1890-1985's.*' Hutton Press. ISBN: 9780907033349

Mann, J. (2010), quoted in *Hansard* (2010), Volume 520: *Football Governance. Debate*. Thursday December 16th 2010 https://tinyurl.com/5c48pf5w

'Mighty, Mighty Whites' website: http://www.mightyleeds.co.uk/players/cawleytom.htm

'Play up Liverpool' website: https://playupliverpool.com/1914/04/28/rochdale-v-liverpool-reserves-2-2/

Rangers Notes in *Liverpool Echo*, December 7th 1945, p.3-6

'Spurs Odyssey' website: https://www.spursodyssey.com/5051/pushandrun.html

Stocks, J. (2017), '*Worksop Town Football Club Volume One: The Early Years - From Shamrocks to Tigers.*' Self-published

Stocks, J. (2018), '*Worksop Town Football Club Volume Two: Renaissance & Rock and Roll 1930-1970.*' Self-published

Stocks, J. (2019), '*Worksop Town Football Club Volume Three: Marching to the Millennium 1970-2000.*' Self-published